New Creation Image

By A.L. and Joyce Gill

ISBN 0-941975-32-0

*Powerhouse Publishing
P.O. Box 99
Fawnskin, CA 92333
(909) 866-3119*

Books By A.L. and Joyce Gill

God's Promises For Your Every Need
Destined for Dominion
Out! In the Name of Jesus
Victory Over Deception

Manuals In This Series

Authority of the Believer
How to Quit Losing
and Start Winning

Church Triumphant
Through the Book of Acts

God's Provision for Healing
Receiving and Ministering
God's Healing Power

The Ministry Gifts
Apostle, Prophet, Evangelist,
Pastor, Teacher

Miracle Evangelism
God's Plan to Reach the World

Patterns for Living
From the Old Testament

Praise and Worship
Becoming Worshipers of God

Supernatural Living
Through the Gifts of the
Holy Spirit

About The Authors

A.L. and Joyce Gill are internationally known speakers, authors and Bible teachers. A.L.'s apostolic ministry travels have taken him to over fifty nations of the world, preaching to crowds exceeding one hundred thousand in person and to many millions by radio and television.

Their top-selling books and manuals have sold over two million copies in the United States. Their writings, which have been translated into many languages, are being used in Bible schools and seminars around the world.

The powerful life-changing truths of God's Word explode in the lives of others through their dynamic preaching, teaching, writing and video and audio tape ministry.

The awesome glory of the presence of God is experienced in their praise and worship seminars as believers discover how to become true and intimate worshipers of God. Many have discovered a new and exciting dimension of victory and boldness through their teachings on the authority of the believer.

The Gills have trained many believers to step into their own God-given supernatural ministries with the healing power of God flowing through their hands. Many have learned to be supernaturally natural as they are released to operate in all nine gifts of the Holy Spirit in their daily lives and ministries.

Both A.L. and Joyce have Master of Theological Studies degrees. A.L. has also earned a Doctor of Philosophy in Theology degree from Vision Christian University. Their ministry in solidly based on the Word of God, is centered on Jesus, strong in faith and taught in the power of the Holy Spirit.

Their ministry is a demonstration of the Father's heart of love. Their preaching and teaching are accompanied by powerful anointing, signs, wonders, and healing miracles with many being slain in waves under the power of God.

Signs of revival including waves of holy laughter, weeping before the Lord and awesome manifestations of God's glory and power are being experienced by many who attend their meetings.

A Word To Teachers And Students

Jesus said, "It is finished!" The redemptive work of Jesus was complete. Why then, do we see so many people living in defeat? Why are so many believers living in sickness? Why are God's people in bondage to demonic forces?

Satan has deceived us! Over a period of time, we have lost the truth of the wonderful things that are included in our redemption. The apostle Paul wrote:

> **Therefore, if anyone is in Christ, he is a new creation; old things have passed away; behold, all things have become new.** *2 Corinthians 5:17*

The life-changing revelation in this study of the **New Creation Image** will free believers from feelings of guilt, condemnation, unworthiness, inferiority, and inadequacy so that they can be conformed to the image of Christ. It will release believers to enjoy being, doing and having all they were created in God's image to be, to do, and to have.

This study will reveal the powerful truths of what it means to be a new creation in Jesus Christ. They are foundational truths which are a "must" for every believer.

The more you saturate yourself with the truths of God's Word concerning the new creation, the more these truths will move from your mind into your spirit. This manual will then provide the outline for you to use as you impart these truths to others.

Personal life illustrations are needed for effective teaching. The authors have omitted these from this work so that the teacher will provide illustrations from his or her own rich experiences, or those of others to which the students will be able to relate. It should always be remembered that it is the Holy Spirit who has come to teach us all things, and that when we are studying, or when we are teaching, we should always be empowered and led by the Holy Spirit.

This study is excellent for personal or group studies, Bible schools, Sunday schools, and home groups. It is important that both the teacher and the students have copies of this manual in hand during the course of the study. Quantity discounts are available.

The best books are written in, underlined, meditated on, and digested. We have left space for your notes and comments. The format has been designed with a fast reference system for review and to assist you in finding areas again. The special format makes it possible for each person, once they have studied through this material, to teach the contents to others. Paul wrote to Timothy:

> **And the things you have heard me say in the presence of many witnesses entrust to reliable men who will also be qualified to teach others.** *2 Timothy 2:2b*

This course is designed as a practical participation Bible course in the MINDS (Ministry Development System) format, which is a specially developed approach to programmed learning. This concept is designed for multiplication in the lives, the ministry and the future teaching of the students. Former students, by using this manual, can teach this course easily to others.

Table of Contents

Lesson One

Created in His Image

Introduction

The study of the **New Creation Image** will bring a powerful revelation of who we are in Christ – what it means to be a new creation. It will bring freedom from feelings of guilt, condemnation, inadequacy, and inferiority. It will boldly release us into an exciting, life-changing revelation of what it means to be one with Jesus Christ.

We will discover what God intended us to be through His great redemptive work. We will find ourselves revealed as:

➢ *Born Again*

➢ *A Recreated Spirit*

➢ *A New Creation*

The apostle Paul wrote these words:
2 Corinthians 5:17 Therefore, if anyone is in Christ, he is a new creation; old things have passed away; behold, all things have become new.

As believers, we are a new race of human beings, a race of "born again" beings with the life of God within us. We are new creations in Christ. Often in this study, believers will be referred to as "new creations."

This study will bring a fresh revelation of who Jesus is and who we are in Him.

With this powerful revelation, we as believers will begin to walk in an exciting new dimension of freedom, authority, boldness, power, and victory in our lives and ministries.

We will find ourselves boldly declaring:

I know who I am in Jesus Christ!
I am what He says I am!
I can do what He says I can do!
I can have what He says I can have!

MANKIND – CREATED IN GOD'S IMAGE

To understand what we are as new creations, we must understand what men and women were first created to be. We must understand that God had a purpose and a plan when He created men and women in His own image and gave them complete authority over this earth.

Genesis 1:26-28 Then God said, "Let Us make man in Our image, according to Our likeness; let them have dominion over the fish of the sea, over the birds of the air, and over the cattle, over all the earth and over every creeping thing that creeps on the earth."

So God created man in His own image; in the image of God He created him; male and female He created them.

Then God blessed them, and God said to them, "Be fruitful and multiply; fill the earth and subdue it; have dominion over the fish of the sea, over the birds of the air, and over every living thing that moves on the earth."

An Image

We were created in the image of God. As new creations, we are being conformed to the image of His Son. An image is an exact likeness. According to **Webster's Unabridged Dictionary**, the word "image" means:

> *An imitation or representation of a person*

> *The visual impression of something produced by reflection from a mirror*

> *A person very much like another; a copy; a counterpart; or a likeness*

> *A vivid representation*

God created Adam in His exact likeness. He created him to be just like God – a mirror reflection of God in his physical body, in his God-like soul, and in his spirit, which was alive with the life and breath of God.

Mankind was created to be the image and glory of God on this earth.

1 Corinthians 11:7a For a man indeed ought not to cover his head, since he is the image and glory of God.

A Triune Being

God said, "Let Us make man in Our image." He said "Our" because God, even though He's one God, is manifested in three distinct personalities.

> *God the Father*

> *God the Son*

> *God the Holy Spirit*

Men and women were created in His image also as triune beings.

> **We are a spirit.**
> *Our spirit is the God-conscious part of us which has to do with the spirit realm – the part of us that can have a relationship and fellowship with God.*

> **We have a soul.**
> *Our soul is the part of us which has to do with the mental realm. It is our intellect, our emotions, our will. It is that part of us which reasons and thinks.*

> **We live in a body.**
> *Our body is the physical part of us – the house in which our spirits and souls live.*

Just as the three persons of the Godhead are separate and distinct, and yet they are one God, in the same way our spirit, soul, and body comprise the real person that God created us to be.

The apostle Paul referred to our triune being when he wrote,

1 Thessalonians 5:23 Now may the God of peace Himself sanctify you completely; and may your whole spirit, soul, and body be preserved blameless at the coming of our Lord Jesus Christ.

We need to have a revelation of our newly created spirit, and through that revelation, God will restore our souls and bodies to once again be all they were created to be. By so doing, we will be "sanctified completely" and "preserved blameless at the coming of our Lord Jesus."

With The Life of God

We know that God, with His own hands, formed Adam in His own image and then breathed into him His breath of life.

Genesis 2:7 And the Lord God formed man of the dust of the ground, and breathed into his nostrils the breath of life; and man became a living being.

The life of God is more than the state of being alive. It is the source of all life.

> *Zoe Life*

There are two important Greek words used for "life" in the New Testament. "Psuche" means natural or human life. "Zoe" means the life and nature of God Himself. It is the Zoe life, the life and nature of God, that has been imparted into every born again believer.

How exciting this is – we are alive with the life and nature of God! When Adam and Eve sinned, they lost the Zoe life of God, but when we are born again, our spirits are made alive with the life of God.

Only the life of God has the power to create. In the creation of man, the dust of the earth became alive because the life of God was breathed into it.

John 1:3,4 All things were made through Him, and without Him nothing was made that was made. In Him was life, and the life was the light of men.

> *With Light of God*

The life of God is light; and this light, or radiant glory, became the light of Adam and Eve before they sinned.

1 John 1:5 This is the message which we have heard from Him and declare to you, that God is light and in Him is no darkness at all.

It is very possible before the fall, that Adam and Eve were clothed in this light from God – His radiant glory.

> *With Perfection of God*

We know Adam and Eve's bodies contained perfect health, power, and strength because these are part of the life of God.

The life-breath of God was flowing through their blood to every cell, giving them perfect health and eternal life. Adam and Eve were created to live forever. They couldn't die as long as they had the life of God within them.

Adam and Eve's souls (minds, emotions, and wills) were God-like in their nature. Their souls had the life of God in them, and their minds, wills, and emotions were one with God.

Their spirits were perfect – one with God.

Given Dominion

The first thing God said about Adam and Eve after He created them was, "Let them have dominion!"

Genesis 1:26 Then God said, "Let Us make man in Our image, according to Our likeness; let them have dominion over the fish of the sea, over the birds of the air, and over the cattle, over all the earth and over every creeping thing that creeps on the earth."

God gave Adam and Eve absolute authority and dominion to rule on this earth. God retained authority and dominion to rule all the universe except on planet earth. Here, He gave this authority to His new creation whom He had created to be just like Himself.

With Power to Create

Just as God's power created the universe, Adam and Eve were given the power to imagine, believe, and create.

Since their wills were one with God, there was no danger of the creative life of God within them being misused for wrongful purposes. All of God's creation on this earth was complete and perfect and they were instructed to multiply that which had already been created perfect.

Genesis 1:28 Then God blessed them, and God said to them, "Be fruitful and multiply; fill the earth and subdue it; have dominion over the fish of the sea, over the birds of the air, and over every living thing that moves on the earth."

Having Fellowship with God

When God created Adam and Eve, they had perfect fellowship with Him. He talked to them face to face. They could boldly approach God. They had no feelings of guilt, condemnation, or inferiority. They had a perfect relationship with God.

God demonstrated His confident trust in Adam as He brought the animals to him so that he could name them.

Genesis 2:19 Out of the ground the Lord God formed every beast of the field and every bird of the air, and brought them to Adam to see what he would call them. And whatever Adam called each living creature, that was its name.

Free Volition

God also gave Adam and Eve a choice – a free will – a free volition. They weren't created as robots without the ability to choose for or against God. They had the ability to choose to obey or disobey.

This choice centered around God's instructions regarding one particular tree in the Garden of Eden, the tree of the knowledge of good and evil. God said that if they ate of that tree, they would surely die.

Genesis 2:16,17 And the Lord God commanded the man, saying, "Of every tree of the garden you may freely eat; but of the tree of the knowledge of good and evil you shall not eat, for in the day that you eat of it you shall surely die."

ENTRANCE OF SIN — MANKIND'S LOSS

The Scripture reveals that Adam and Eve chose to disobey God. This was sin.

Genesis 3:6 So when the woman saw that the tree was good for food, that it was pleasant to the eyes, and a tree desirable to make one wise, she took of its fruit and ate. She also gave to her husband with her, and he ate.

Through sin, all humanity suffered tremendous loss.

Loss of Fellowship

God in His perfect holiness and righteousness could no longer fellowship with Adam and Eve. Their sin became a barrier between them and God. Their guilt and condemnation caused them to hide from God.

Genesis 3:8 And they heard the sound of the Lord God walking in the garden in the cool of the day, and Adam and his wife hid themselves from the presence of the Lord God among the trees of the garden.

They had lost their most precious possessions, their relationship and perfect fellowship with God.

Loss of the Life of God

When Adam and Eve ate the forbidden fruit, they died spiritually. They no longer had the life of God within them.

Romans 5:12 Therefore, just as through one man sin entered the world, and death through sin, and thus death spread to all men, because all sinned. Their spirits became spiritually dead. Their spirits became inoperative. The breath of God's spirit, which God had breathed into Adam, was no longer there.

Loss of God's Glory

The glory of God that was Adam and Eve's covering was suddenly gone.

Romans 3:23 For all have sinned and fall short of the glory of God ...

They suddenly realized that they were naked.

Genesis 3:7a Then the eyes of both of them were opened, and they knew that they were naked.

Loss of Spiritual Perception

When Adam and Eve became spiritually dead, their souls were no longer alive to God. Their thoughts were no longer God's thoughts. Their source of perception moved from their spirit, which was now dead, to what they could sense through their natural bodies.

They began to operate in the natural realm through their five senses. Reality and truth became what they could see, hear, smell, taste, or touch.

Loss of Perfect Health

The bodies of Adam and Eve no longer had the life of God flowing through their veins. They were now subject to sickness, disease, and deterioration. At the moment they sinned, they began to age and die physically.

Loss of Authority

Adam and Eve lost their authority and dominion over this earth. They surrendered it to Satan. They were now living in his kingdom, hopelessly subject to the one who had come to "steal, kill, and destroy."

Became Unregenerate

An unregenerate mind, and a believer's mind which hasn't been renewed by the Word of God, are often full of wicked imaginations.

Proverbs 6:16,17,18 (King James Version KJV) These six things doth the LORD hate: yea, seven are an abomination unto him: a proud look, a lying tongue, and hands that shed innocent blood, an heart that deviseth wicked imaginations, feet that be swift in running to mischief ...

They are full of the things God hates.

> ➢ *Pride*

> ➢ *Lying Tongues*

> ➢ *Shedding Innocent Blood*

> ➢ *Devising Wicked Imaginations*

> ➢ *Running to Mischief*

The apostle Paul also describes the ungodly, unrighteous person.

Romans 1:18-22 For the wrath of God is revealed from heaven against all ungodliness and unrighteousness of men, who suppress the truth in unrighteousness, because what may be known of God is manifest in them, for God has shown it to them.

For since the creation of the world His invisible attributes are clearly seen, being understood by the things that are made, even His eternal power and Godhead, so that they are without excuse, because, although they knew God, they did not glorify Him as God, nor were thankful, but became futile in their thoughts, and their foolish hearts were darkened.

Professing to be wise, they became fools.

PROMISE OF THE REDEEMER

The First Promise

Adam and Eve stood in the Garden of Eden:

➤ *Hopelessly stripped of their relationship and fellowship with God*

➤ *Stripped of their authority*

➤ *Stripped of their perfect wisdom and health*

However, when God spoke to Satan, He promised mankind's restoration through the substitutionary work of a Redeemer who would be the seed of the woman.

Genesis 3:15 And I will put enmity between you and the woman, and between your seed and her Seed; He shall bruise your head, and you shall bruise His heel.

Through Seed of Abraham

The promise of the Redeemer was renewed when God said that all the nations of the world would be blessed through Abraham.

Genesis 18:18 Abraham shall surely become a great and mighty nation, and all the nations of the earth shall be blessed in him.

God repeated this covenant promise to Isaac and Jacob. He promised that all nations of the earth would be blessed through their seed. There was a coming Redeemer!

Through Seed of David

God also made a covenant promise to David regarding his seed. This too, was a reference to the coming Redeemer, Jesus Christ.

Psalms 89:34-36a My covenant will I not break, nor alter the thing that is gone out of my lips. Once have I sworn by my holiness that I will not lie unto David. His seed shall endure for ever.

Prophesied by Isaiah

Isaiah prophesied the coming Redeemer.

Isaiah 9:6,7a For unto us a Child is born, unto us a Son is given; and the government will be upon His shoulder. And His name will be called Wonderful, Counselor, Mighty God, Everlasting Father, Prince of Peace. Of the increase of His government and peace there will be no end, upon the throne of David and over His kingdom, to order it and establish it with judgment and justice from that time forward, even forever.

Our Substitute

Sin and death were the results of the rebellion of Adam and Eve. It was only through the coming of the last Adam as our Substitute, that we could be set free of these penalties. Isaiah fifty-three gives us a wonderful picture of the coming Redeemer.

Isaiah 53:4,5 Surely He has borne our griefs and carried our sorrows; yet we esteemed Him stricken, smitten by God, and afflicted. But He was wounded for our transgressions, He was bruised for our iniquities; the chastisement for our peace was upon Him, and by His stripes we are healed.

Through the substitutionary redemptive work of the coming Messiah, all that Adam and Eve had lost in the fall would be restored. Once again mankind could become all they were created to be. The new creation would be restored!

QUESTIONS:

1. Why did Adam and Eve have so many God-like characteristics when they were created?

2. What did Adam and Eve have on the inside that made them so different from the other animals that God created?

3. List some of the things that mankind lost in the fall that would be restored to the new creation.

Lesson Two

Our Image of the Father

Introduction

To understand our new creation image, we must have a revelation of who God the Father is. Since we were created in His image, we can never understand who we were created to be until we have a true image of the Father.

The apostle Paul wrote, that as we behold the glory of the Lord, we will be transformed into the same image. Revelation brings transformation.

2 Corinthians 3:18 But we all, with unveiled face, beholding as in a mirror the glory of the Lord, are being transformed into the same image from glory to glory, just as by the Spirit of the Lord.

In this lesson, we are going to behold the glory of the Father. We are going to reject erroneous images we may have of the Father. We are going to allow the Holy Spirit, by the revelation of God's Word, to reveal a true image of our loving heavenly Father.

Three Moves of the Spirit

➢ *Jesus People*

In the Jesus People Movement, many received a fresh revelation and came into an intimate relationship and fellowship with the Person of Jesus.

➢ *Charismatic Renewal*

In the Charismatic Renewal, many came into an intimate relationship and fellowship with the Person of the Holy Spirit.

As people were led by the Holy Spirit, they laid aside the old hymn books and discovered the joy of entering into the Biblical expressions of praise to Jesus.

David expressed this for us when he wrote,
Psalm 100:4 Enter into His gates with thanksgiving, and into His courts with praise. Be thankful to Him, and bless His name.

➢ *Knowing the Father*

In this present move of God before the soon return of Jesus, we are going to come into an intimate relationship and fellowship with the Father. We are going to become worshipers of Him.

We have been singing, raising our hands, clapping, shouting, leaping, and dancing before the Lord in the courtyard. However, now there is coming an overwhelming desire to enter into the Father's presence inside the Holy of Holies – to enter within the veil.

No longer are we satisfied to remain in the courtyard. We long to seek the face of our Father, to look into His eyes, to feel His arms of love around us, and to become intimate with Him in worship.

John 4:23 But the hour is coming, and now is, when the true worshipers will worship the Father in spirit and truth; for the Father is seeking such to worship Him.

The Father is seeking true worshipers who will spend time worshiping Him in spirit and in truth, who will enter into the Holy of Holies.

OUR EARTHLY FATHER

Our image of our heavenly Father is often established by the characteristics of our earthly fathers. Our relationships with our earthly fathers affect our relationships with the heavenly Father.

Too Busy

Many fathers were too busy to spend time with their children as they were growing up. This may have been for very good reasons, but this has left many with the feeling "God is too busy for me."

Stern Disciplinarian

Some fathers have dealt harshly with their children using stern discipline without showing love. These children often feel their heavenly Father is looking down with a stern, disapproving look on His face as though He has a club in His hand just waiting for someone to get out of line.

Lack of Love

Many have grown up in homes where very little love or attention was shown to them by their fathers. No matter how hard they tried, it seems they were never able to receive approval or recognition from their fathers.

To these, the image of their heavenly Father is one of disapproval and indifference to their needs. They feel God is uncaring about their accomplishments and that He doesn't really love them.

Poverty

Others were raised in families where their fathers either couldn't, or didn't, provide an adequate income to properly support the family with the basic needs of life. They grew up in poverty.

These people often have a "poverty image" of God. They have difficulty believing God will supply every need of their life.

Abuse

Many children have been abused by their earthly fathers. Some have been abused emotionally, others physically, and still others have suffered the trauma of sexual abuse.

This has prevented them from being able to fully trust their heavenly Father or to receive His great love and affection. They feel guilty before God or angry with Him, and they are unable to fully trust Him with their lives.

OUR HEAVENLY FATHER

Love

Regardless of the hurts, rejection, or abuse that we may have received from our earthly fathers, we must forgive them, and receive healing from God so that we can know, receive, and enjoy the overwhelming love of our heavenly Father.

1 John 3:1a Behold what manner of love the Father has bestowed on us, that we should be called children of God!

The apostle Paul wrote that nothing could separate us from the Father's love.

Romans 8:38,39 For I am persuaded that neither death nor life, nor angels nor principalities nor powers, nor things present nor things to come, nor height nor depth, nor any other created thing, shall be able to separate us from the love of God which is in Christ Jesus our Lord.

Father Rejoices over Us

Instead of a stern, uncaring father, we have a heavenly Father who loves us so much that He is rejoicing over us with gladness and with singing.

The prophet Zephaniah describes God this way:
Zephaniah 3:17 The LORD your God in your midst, the Mighty One, will save; He will rejoice over you with gladness, He will quiet you in His love, He will rejoice over you with singing.

The Hebrew word Zephaniah used for rejoice has the primary meaning of "springing" or "leaping." God is so delighted in us as His children, He jumps up and down and dances in a joyful expression of overwhelming pleasure.

What a different image of the Father this is! God isn't too busy for us. He isn't a stern, unloving disciplinarian. He isn't interested in punishing us. He is rejoicing over us with singing. He is leaping up and down in joy over us!

Hearts Turned to Father

Today, even as in the Old Testament, God is using the prophets to turn the hearts of the children to their fathers.

Malachi 4:5,6a Behold, I will send you Elijah the prophet before the coming of the great and dreadful day of the LORD. And he will turn the hearts of the fathers to the children, and the hearts of the children to their fathers.

God is turning the hearts of sons and daughters to their earthly fathers and the hearts of His sons and daughters of God to their heavenly Father.

THREE HINDRANCES TO FELLOWSHIP

Sin

Adam and Even had perfect fellowship with God until the moment they sinned. A holy and righteous God couldn't have fellowship with sin.

At the moment of salvation, our sins are forgiven and removed. Our relationship, and fellowship with God begins. If we sin, even though our relationship with God continues, our fellowship with Him is broken. This fellowship can only be restored by confessing our sins to Him.

1 John 1:9 If we confess our sins, He is faithful and just to forgive us our sins and to cleanse us from all unrighteousness.

Rejection

Many were rejected by their earthly fathers. They may have been the result of an unplanned or unwanted pregnancy. Perhaps the father wanted a child of the opposite sex, or as a child, they didn't measure up to their father's expectations.

Whether a person suffered actual rejection or unwarranted feelings of rejection, great emotional scars have been left in that person's life.

These people often feel that their heavenly Father is also rejecting them. They have difficulty receiving His love and acceptance. Something always seems to prevent them from coming into a close personal relationship with their heavenly Father and becoming a true worshiper of Him.

A person who has feelings of rejection in their life must forgive those who have rejected them and then receive God's healing power into their souls.

Fear

Fear of coming into the Father's presence has kept many from becoming true worshipers of Him. However, instead of fear, God has given us a Spirit of adoption by which we can come to Him and call Him "Abba Father."

Romans 8:15 For you did not receive the spirit of bondage again to fear, but you received the Spirit of adoption by whom we cry out, "Abba, Father."

"Abba" is an expression of endearment, of close personal relationship with our Father. It could be translated, "Daddy."

2 Corinthians 6:18 I will be a Father to you, and you shall be My sons and daughters, says the Lord Almighty.

It was only by the Father's overwhelming love for us that He adopted us to be His children.

1 John 3:1a Behold what manner of love the Father has bestowed on us, that we should be called children of God!

An understanding of God's tremendous love for us removes our fear.

David, Our Example

David was a man who had a heart after God. He desired to become intimate with his heavenly Father in worship.

Psalm 27:4 One thing I have desired of the LORD, that will I seek: that I may dwell in the house of the LORD all the days of my life, to behold the beauty of the LORD, and to inquire in His temple.

David desired to dwell in God's presence every day of his life. He desired to enter into the presence of the Father, and to look on His beauty.

➤ *Offered Praise and Worship*

Psalm 27:6b I will offer sacrifices of joy in His tabernacle; I will sing, yes, I will sing praises to the LORD.

David knew how to sing praises and dance before the Lord in the "courtyards." However, he desired more. He desired to enter into the very presence of the Father and to seek His face.

Psalm 27:8 When You said, "Seek My face," my heart said to You, "Your face, LORD, I will seek."

➤ *Feared Rejection by God*

Even as much as David desired to worship the Father, as he began to enter the presence of the Father in intimate worship, he suddenly drew back with fear of rejection.

Psalm 27:9 Do not hide Your face from me; do not turn Your servant away in anger; You have been my help; do not leave me nor forsake me, O God of my salvation.

➤ *Rejection by Earthly Father*

David had suffered rejection from his earthly father as a boy, and now that same fear of rejection was keeping him from entering his heavenly Father's presence without fear.

When David was a young man, the prophet Samuel came to Bethlehem to anoint the next king. David's father had gathered all of his other sons together in hopes that one of them would be anointed to be king. David wasn't invited to appear before Samuel on that important day.

This could have been a time when David felt deep rejection by his earthly father. This created a fear in David's heart that he would also be rejected by his heavenly Father.

As much as he desired to come into his heavenly Father's presence, to seek His face, and to behold His beauty, at the moment he began to enter into deep worship, the fear of rejection gripped his soul.

➤ *Freed From Rejection*

David realized he had been rejected by his father and mother. He understood the problem, and then he made a strong declaration against that feeling of rejection.

Psalm 27:10 When my father and my mother forsake me, then the LORD will take care of me.

At that moment, David walked confidently into the presence of God. He looked into His face and felt the love and acceptance of His Father flood his spirit.

JESUS REVEALS HIS FATHER

One of the main purposes of Jesus' time on this earth was to reveal His Father. As the earthly ministry of Jesus was coming to an end, immediately before His arrest, trial, and crucifixion, Jesus mentioned His Father fifty times in the Gospel of John, chapters fourteen through seventeen.

He said over and over again to His disciples, "I want you to know my Father!"

"Know Me - Know Father"

If we know Jesus, we will know the Father. The more we spend time knowing Jesus through the Gospels, the more we will know the Father.

John 14:7 If you had known Me, you would have known My Father also; and from now on you know Him and have seen Him.

In the Gospels, we see the love and compassion of Jesus as he was continually reaching out and touching people, meeting their needs, healing their bodies, and restoring their souls. This was an expression of the Father's love.

John 14:9b He who has seen Me has seen the Father.

> ### *The Father's Love*

When Jesus took the children up on His lap and put His arms around them, He demonstrated the Father's love for His children.

Matthew 19:14 But Jesus said, "Let the little children come to Me, and do not forbid them; for of such is the kingdom of heaven."

What a wonderful picture this is of how much our Father would love to draw us close to Himself and put His arms around us.

As Jesus ministered to those around Him, He revealed His Father's love.

John 14:23 Jesus answered and said to him, "If anyone loves Me, he will keep My word; and My Father will love him, and We will come to him and make Our home with him."

What a powerful revelation this is. Say it out loud.

> *My heavenly Father loves me!*
> *He wants to come with Jesus and live with me!*
> *My Father wants to make His home with me!*

> ### *The Father's Giving*

Jesus said that we can confidently ask our Father for provision.

John 16:23b Most assuredly, I say to you, whatever you ask the Father in My name He will give you.

We don't ask in Jesus' name because the Father loves Jesus and will only do things for Him. We ask in Jesus' name because it is through the sacrifice of Jesus that our relationship with the Father is restored.

➤ *The Father's House*

Jesus told us about His Father's house. He said that He would go and prepare a place for us in His Father's house.

John 14:2 In My Father's house are many mansions (rooms); if it were not so, I would have told you. I go to prepare a place for you.

In the future, we are to live in the Father's house. This is where the family lives. We are to have an intimate relationship with our heavenly Father.

"I'll Tell You Plainly"

Jesus wants to tell us plainly about His Father.

John 16:25 These things I have spoken to you in figurative language; but the time is coming when I will no longer speak to you in figurative language, but I will tell you plainly about the Father.

These are only a few of the fifty times Jesus mentioned His Father in these four chapters. Jesus expressed His great desire that each one of us would come into an intimate relationship with His Father.

PRODIGAL SON

Often the parable of the Prodigal Son is used in evangelistic messages as a call for repentance or restoration to fellowship. We have understood that we could come to the Father no matter how low we had sunk.

In rebellion, the prodigal son had left home and squandered all of his inheritance in wild living. Then when a severe famine came, he ended up feeding pigs and longing to eat the pods that the pigs were eating.

The Son

Most of us can identify with the son. We have felt, or may feel, alienated from our heavenly Father, fearful of rejection, or full of feelings of unworthiness, remorse, and guilt.

Luke 15:17-20a But when he came to himself, he said, "How many of my father's hired servants have bread enough and to spare, and I perish with hunger!

"I will arise and go to my father, and will say to him, 'Father, I have sinned against heaven and before you, and I am no longer worthy to be called your son. Make me like one of your hired servants.'"

He said, "I am no longer worthy." This young man, even as so many believers today, felt unworthy. He had an unworthy image of himself. But even with that self-image, he did come home.

The Father

This parable is a wonderful revelation of our heavenly Father.

> *He wasn't judgmental.*
> *He wasn't stern.*
> *He didn't wait for his son to beg*
> *for forgiveness.*

What did Jesus say he did?
Luke 15:20b But when he was still a great way off, his father saw him and had compassion, and ran and fell on his neck and kissed him.

Instead of our Father turning His face away from us in rejection, He is waiting for us to come to Him. He wants to put His arms around us and kiss us as an expression of His great and overwhelming love.

v. 21 And the son said to him, "Father, I have sinned against heaven and in your sight, and am no longer worthy to be called your son."

The father didn't even discuss what the son had done, or what he was then saying.

vs. 22-24 But the father said to his servants, "Bring out the best robe and put it on him, and put a ring on his hand and sandals on his feet. And bring the fatted calf here and kill it, and let us eat and be merry; for this my son was dead and is alive again; he was lost and is found." And they began to be merry.

Son's Image

The father knew that he had to change his son's self-image. He put his best robe on him. He put his ring on his finger and a new pair of sandals on his feet.

Once we have accepted Jesus as our Savior, our heavenly Father looks on us as sons and daughters. We are dressed in His robes of righteousness. We have His ring of authority on our fingers.

In love, He is saying, "Oh, how I want them to know who they are in Jesus Christ. They are one with my Son! They are the righteousness of God in Jesus Christ."

The apostle Paul wrote about this.
2 Corinthians 5:21 For He (God) made Him who knew no sin to be sin for us, that we might become the righteousness of God in Him.

Our New Creation Image

As we allow Jesus to reveal His Father to us, any distorted or limited images we have of our heavenly Father will change.

We will, like David, behold the beauty of the Lord. We will seek His face. We will become worshipers of Him. We will feel His acceptance all around us. As we behold the glory of the Lord, our image of the Father will change, and at the same time our old self-image will be changed into a new creation image.

Many have been seeking God's hand instead of seeking His face. They have been spending their time in coming to God to get their own needs met.

Transformed

> ### *By Seeking the Father*

Instead we are to come to God and spend time in seeking His face and beholding His glory. Then, we will be transformed into His image.

2 Corinthians 3:18 But we all, with unveiled face, beholding as in a mirror the glory of the Lord, are being transformed into the same image from glory to glory, just as by the Spirit of the Lord.

The psalmist David expressed the same thought as the apostle Paul.

Psalm 17:15 As for me, I will see your face in righteousness; I shall be satisfied when I awake in Your likeness.

> ### *By Worshiping the Father*

We aren't changed into His likeness by looking to ourselves and desiring that transformation to take place in our lives. We are changed into His likeness as we spend time with our Father in intimate love and worship of Him for who He is.

As we continue to spend time seeking the face of God, we will "awake" to find that our faces will glow with the glory of God. We, like Moses when he came down from spending time with God on Mount Sinai, will radiate with the glory of God.

Luke wrote,

Luke 11:36 (Tyndale Living Bible TLB) **If you are filled with light within, with no dark corners, then your face will be radiant too, as though a floodlight is beamed upon you.**

Once again, we will become what humanity was created to be when God said, "Let us make man in our image."

QUESTIONS:

1. How is our image of our heavenly Father affected by our childhood experiences?

2. How can our image of our heavenly Father be changed to agree with the true Father image revealed in God's Word?

3. According to 2 Corinthians 3:18, how can we be transformed into the image of the Lord?

Lesson Three

Our Image of the Son

THE SON OF GOD

To have a full revelation of who we are as new creations, we must have a revelation of the image of the Son of God.

The apostle Paul wrote that God predestined, determined, or ordained us to be conformed to the image of the Son of God.

Romans 8:29a For whom He foreknew, He also predestined to be conformed to the image of His Son.

As we are conformed to the image of His Son, we will begin to fulfill our potential and live as new creation beings. We know Jesus is one with the Father and with the Holy Spirit, and that every attribute they have – we have.

Is God

The apostle John tells us four important things about the Son of God.

> *He always existed.*

> *He is the Living Word of God.*

> *He is the creator of all things.*

> *He became flesh and dwelt among us.*

John 1:1-3,14 In the beginning was the Word, and the Word was with God, and the Word was God. He was in the beginning with God. All things were made through Him, and without Him nothing was made that was made.

And the Word became flesh and dwelt among us.

Created Adam and Eve

John made it clear that everything was created by the Son of God. Adam and Eve were created by Him.

Genesis 1:27 So God created man in His own image; in the image of God He created him; male and female He created them.

Redeemed mankind is to be re-created, to be conformed to the image of the one who created Adam and Eve in His own image.

THE SON OF MAN

Gave up Rights as God

Jesus was born of a virgin on this earth as a human being. He was still truly God, but He gave up His rights as God and came to this earth as a man. He was true humanity, but undiminished Deity.

Philippians 2:5-8 Let this mind be in you which was also in Christ Jesus, Who, being in the form of God, did not consider it robbery to be equal with God, but made Himself of no reputation, taking the form of a servant, and coming in the likeness of men. And being found in appearance as a man, He humbled Himself and became obedient to the point of death, even the death of the cross.

It is very important to understand that Jesus laid aside His rights as God. He made Himself as a man. Everything Jesus did while He lived and ministered on this earth, He did as man, not as God.

False Conception

If we picture Jesus as He walked on this earth operating in His power as God, we cannot understand how we can be conformed to His image.

"Yes!" we would say, "Jesus could heal the sick, cast out demons, and still the storm. After all, He was the Son of God. He was all powerful! What does that have to do with us?"

How could Jesus be an example or pattern for our lives if He was operating as God? If Jesus lived and ministered in the realm of the supernatural, our excuse is that we are merely human.

"The only hope we have," we would reason, "is to pray for God's supernatural intervention to deliver us out of our struggles, sicknesses, or financial problems."

If we picture Jesus operating on this earth – laying aside His rights as God - coming as a man in the authority which God gave man - then we can picture ourselves doing the same things Jesus did.

Authority on Earth

Jesus said,
John 5:24,25 I tell you the truth, whoever hears my word and believes him who sent me has eternal life and will not be condemned; he has crossed over from death to life. I tell you the truth, a time is coming and has now come when the dead will hear the voice of the Son of God and those who hear will live.

Those that hear the voice of the Son of God, will live.

Then Jesus goes on to say,

John 5:26,27 For as the Father has life in himself, so he has granted the Son to have life in himself. And he has given him authority to judge because he is the Son of Man.

It is obvious from this passage that the authority that Jesus lived and ministered in while He was on this earth, wasn't His authority as the Son of God. It was His authority as the Son of Man.

Jesus is uniquely qualified to be our example. As new creations in Jesus, our God-given authority on this earth has been restored. We are to operate in the same authority as Jesus, the Son of Man, did. When we receive the baptism in the Holy Spirit, we can operate in the same power Jesus did after the Holy Spirit came on Him.

Now, as we read the Gospels, we can see that Jesus was truly our example and pattern. We can operate in the same authority and power Jesus did upon this earth. Mankind, as new creations, can live in the same authority they were created to live in when God said, "Let them have dominion!"

Was Last Adam

Jesus came as the Last Adam.

1 Corinthians 15:45 And so it is written, "The first man Adam became a living being." The last Adam became a life-giving spirit.

Everything Adam was created to do – Jesus did. God said, "Let them have dominion" – Jesus took dominion over demons, over living things, over the elements. He walked in authority.

Matthew 7:28,29 And so it was, when Jesus had ended these sayings, that the people were astonished at His teaching, for He taught them as one having authority, and not as the scribes.

➤ *Shared our Humanity*

Jesus shared in our humanity as flesh and blood.

Hebrews 2:14a Inasmuch then as the children have partaken of flesh and blood, He Himself likewise shared in the same.

➤ *Experienced Temptations*

He experienced the same temptations we do.

Hebrews 4:15 For we do not have a High Priest who cannot sympathize with our weaknesses, but was in all points tempted as we are, yet without sin.

Even though He had the same temptations as any human, Jesus lived without sin just as Adam and Eve were created to do.

➤ *His Works - Our Works*

Jesus came to be and do all that He had created mankind to be and do. He laid aside His rights as God and lived and ministered as a human being on this earth.

John 14:12 Most assuredly, I say to you, he who believes in Me, the works that I do he will do also; and greater works than these he will do, because I go to My Father.

Jesus wouldn't say, "he who believes will do the same works or even greater works" if this weren't possible.

➤ *His Power - Our Power*

All the powerful works and ministry of Jesus were done in the power of the Holy Spirit.

Luke 3:22a And the Holy Spirit descended in bodily form like a dove upon Him.

There are no recorded miracles of Jesus until after the Holy Spirit came on Him at His baptism. This was the beginning of the earthly ministry of Jesus.

Jesus said He was anointed by the Holy Spirit to preach the gospel, heal the sick, and cast out devils.

Luke 4:18,19 The Spirit of the Lord is upon Me, because He has anointed Me to preach the gospel to the poor. He has sent Me to heal the brokenhearted, to preach deliverance to the captives and recovery of sight to the blind, to set at liberty those who are oppressed, to preach the acceptable year of the Lord.

When Jesus was preparing to leave this earth, He spoke of the coming of the Holy Spirit, and He said that the Holy Spirit would give His followers power.

Acts 1:8a But you will receive power when the Holy Spirit comes on you.

We have the same power which operated in Jesus' life as He ministered on the earth.

Luke used the same words – "power" and "Holy Spirit" – when he wrote about Jesus' life.

Acts 10:38 God anointed Jesus of Nazareth with the Holy Spirit and with power, who went about doing good and healing all who were oppressed by the devil, for God was with Him.

Jesus Came

> ➢ *To Reveal the Father*

Jesus, the Son of God, is the exact image of the Father.

Jesus said,
John 10:30 I and My Father are one.

He also said,
John 14:6,7 I am the way, the truth, and the life. No one comes to the Father except through Me. If you had known Me, you would have known My Father also; and from now on you know Him and have seen Him.

The writer of the book of Hebrews said that Jesus was the express image of God.

Hebrews 1:3a Who being the brightness of His glory and the express image of His person ...

Paul wrote that Christ was the image of the invisible God.

Colossians 1:15 He is the image of the invisible God, the firstborn over all creation.

Jesus was the first-born in the image of His Father to be over all creation. We are born-again to be conformed to His image as new creations.

> ➢ *To Do Father's Will*

As Jesus came to this earth, He surrendered His will to the Father. As He walked on this earth, He did the Father's will.

John 6:38 For I have come down from heaven, not to do My own will, but the will of Him who sent Me.

> ➢ *To Destroy Works of Devil*

Everywhere Jesus ministered, He destroyed the works of the devil. John tells us that this was one of the main reasons He came to this earth.

1 John 3:8b For this purpose the Son of God was manifested, that He might destroy the works of the devil.

JESUS OUR SUBSTITUTE

Sin's Penalty

Adam and Eve's sin left them separated from a Holy God who couldn't coexist with sin. God couldn't decide, in love, to simply overlook sin, because God is also perfect justice. Sin couldn't be tolerated by a holy and just God.

God had said,

Genesis 2:17b ... for in the day that you eat of it you shall surely die.

Adam and Eve lost their relationship with God. The Spirit of God within them couldn't stay when they sinned. Adam and Eve couldn't give to their children what they no longer possessed. The God-nature within them was gone, and a sin-nature had taken its place. Adam's sin-nature was passed on to His descendants.

1 Corinthians 15:22 For as in Adam all die, even so in Christ all shall be made alive.

The sin nature is passed from one generation to another through the seed of the father. Since every person on this earth has a father, the apostle Paul wrote,

Romans 3:23 For all have sinned and fall short of the glory of God.

The penalty for sin was spiritual death, and this resulted in physical death.

Romans 6:23 For the wages of sin is death, but the gift of God is eternal life in Christ Jesus our Lord.

Romans 5:12 Therefore, just as through one man sin entered the world, and death through sin, and thus death spread to all men, because all sinned ...

Birth of Jesus

Jesus came to this earth, conceived by the Holy Spirit and born of a virgin, to become our substitute. Because of His miraculous conception, Jesus didn't have a sin nature. He had the nature of God within Him, which mankind had lost.

Matthew 1:20b Joseph, son of David, do not be afraid to take to you Mary your wife, for that which is conceived in her is of the Holy Spirit.

Matthew 1:23 "Behold, a virgin shall be with child, and bear a Son, and they shall call His name Immanuel," which is translated, "God with us."

God's Love Plan

God's love for mankind is almost inconceivable! Both John and Paul wrote about it.

John 3:16 For God so loved the world that He gave His only begotten Son, that whoever believes in Him should not perish but have everlasting life.

Romans 5:8 But God demonstrates His own love toward us, in that while we were still sinners, Christ died for us.

God's great love plan for mankind included sending His only Son, Jesus, to live as the perfect man, and then for His Son to take on Himself mankind's penalty for sin.

1 Peter 3:18 For Christ also suffered once for sins, the just for the unjust, that He might bring us to God, being put to death in the flesh but made alive by the Spirit.

Jesus took our place. All the judgment we deserved, He took upon Himself. He became sin for us so we might receive His righteousness. He bore our sins so that we don't have to bear them.

2 Corinthians 5:21 For He made Him who knew no sin to be sin for us, that we might become the righteousness of God in Him.

He bore our sicknesses, diseases, and pains so that we don't have to bear them.

Isaiah 53:4 (Amplified Bible) Surely He has borne our griefs-sickness, weakness and distress-and carried our sorrows and pain [of punishment]. Yet we ignorantly considered Him stricken, smitten and afflicted by God [as if with leprosy]. But He was wounded for our transgressions, He was bruised for our guilt and iniquities; the chastisement needful to obtain peace and well-being for us was upon Him, and with the stripes that wounded Him we are healed and made whole.

JESUS - OUR REDEEMER

In the earliest of the Old Testament writings, Job prophesied about the coming Redeemer.

Job 19:25 For I know that my Redeemer lives, and He shall stand at last on the earth.

David wrote,
Psalms 19:14 Let the words of my mouth and the meditation of my heart Be acceptable in Your sight, O LORD, my strength and my redeemer.

Isaiah wrote about the Redeemer over and over.

Isaiah 44:6 Thus says the LORD, the King of Israel, and his Redeemer, the LORD of hosts: 'I am the First and I am the Last; besides Me there is no God.'

Redeemed from Slavery

Throughout the Old Testament, a person in financial difficulty could sell himself or his family into slavery. This person, or persons, could be set free if he was "redeemed" by a kinsman or even by themselves if they could come up with enough money. Sometimes they were set free because of the number of years of service, or due to an unusually courageous act they performed.

The Scriptures view unregenerate mankind as hopeless slaves to sin and to Satan, their master.

By His Blood

Mankind couldn't be redeemed by any corruptible things – not by silver or gold – not by any act they could do. The price of their redemption was the blood of the eternal Son of God who had become flesh. It was a blood of infinite value, a blood so powerful that it was sufficient to cleanse the sins of all mankind.

1 Peter 1:18,19 Knowing that you were not redeemed with corruptible things, like silver or gold, from your aimless conduct received by tradition from your fathers, but with the precious blood of Christ, as of a lamb without blemish and without spot.

To Be Set Free

The Greek word translated "redeemed" in this verse emphasized the act of setting free or liberating by purchase. We, who had been His through the act of creation, now belonged to the Redeemer by purchase.

John 8:36 Therefore if the Son makes you free, you shall be free indeed.

Jesus not only redeemed us, He set us free! He purchased us with His own precious blood. We became His possession, and He had the legal right to set us free.

To be Kings and Priests

The original word "agorazo" translated "redeemed" in the following verse means "to go to the market to purchase." Jesus purchased us out of slavery to be made kings and priests in Him.

Revelation 5:9,10 And they sang a new song, saying: "You are worthy to take the scroll, and to open its seals; for You were slain, and have redeemed us to God by Your blood out of every tribe and tongue and people and nation. And have made us kings and priests to our God; and we shall reign on the earth."

For All Eternity

The compound word, "exagorazo" translated "redeemed" in Galatians 3:13, means "to purchase out of so that it can never return."

Galatians 3:13a Christ has redeemed us from the curse of the law ...

By the redemptive work of Christ on our behalf, we were purchased out of slavery to sin, so completely and effectively, that we can be confident of not being returned to the slave market again.

This was especially meaningful to those of Roman days who could be sold again and again on the auction block by their slave masters.

JESUS – OUR IDENTITY

One with Him

The moment we placed our faith in Jesus as our Savior, a miracle took place. God the Holy Spirit made us one with Him. We became His Body.

1 Corinthians 12:13,17 For by one Spirit we were all baptized into one body–whether Jews or Greeks, whether slaves or free–and have all been made to drink into one Spirit. Now you are the body of Christ, and members individually.

The reason for Jesus' redemptive work wasn't only so that some day we could be with Him in heaven. Peter wrote that Jesus provided a way that we might live for righteousness.

1 Peter 2:22,24 Who committed no sin, nor was guile found in His mouth ... Who Himself bore our sins in His own body on the tree, that we, having died to sins, might live for righteousness-by whose stripes you were healed.

Became Sin for Us

In Jesus' redemptive work on our behalf, He "became" sin for us. He willingly took our sins on His own body on the cross.

2 Corinthians 5:21 For He made Him who knew no sin to be sin for us, that we might become the righteousness of God in Him.

Became Curse for Us

Jesus took on Himself the curse that had come on mankind due to sin.

Galatians 3:13 Christ has redeemed us from the curse of the law, having become a curse for us (for it is written, "Cursed is everyone who hangs on a tree".)

Bore our Sins Away

On the cross, Jesus became "the lamb of God which takes away the sin of the world." He bore all of our sins to the depth of the earth to be remembered by God no more, forever.

John 1:29 The next day John saw Jesus coming toward him, and said, "Behold! The Lamb of God who takes away the sin of the world!"

Psalms 88:3,6,7 For my soul is full of troubles, and my life draws near to the grave.

You have laid me in the lowest pit, in darkness, in the depths. Your wrath lies heavy upon me, and You have afflicted me with all Your waves.

We became one with Him in His death.

Romans 6:6 Knowing this, that our old man was crucified with Him, that the body of sin might be done away with, that we should no longer be slaves of sin.

Was Made Alive

Having delivered our sins to the depth of the earth, He rose triumphant over death, hell, and the grave. He became the "first-born from the dead."

Colossians 1:18 And He is the head of the body, the church, who is the beginning, the firstborn from the dead, that in all things He may have the preeminence.

He was "made alive" by the Spirit.

1 Peter 3:18 For Christ also suffered once for sins, the just for the unjust, that He might bring us to God, being put to death in the flesh but made alive by the Spirit.

When Jesus was made alive, we were made alive with Him.

Ephesians 2:5,6 Even when we were dead in trespasses, made us alive together with Christ (by grace you have been saved), and raised us up together, and made us sit together in the heavenly places in Christ Jesus ...

When Jesus was made alive, He was restored to the full life and nature of The Father. He was once again made righteous.

Romans 3:26 To demonstrate at the present time His righteousness, that He might be just and the justifier of the one who has faith in Jesus.

Became our Righteousness

At the moment of salvation, we were given the righteousness of Jesus. We became just as righteous as Jesus is righteous.

Paul wrote,
2 Corinthians 5:21 For He made Him who knew no sin to be sin for us, that we might become the righteousness of God in Him.

Now we who have been made righteous are to "live for righteousness."

Peter wrote,
1 Peter 2:24a Who Himself bore our sins in His own body on the tree, that we, having died to sins, might live for righteousness.

As new creations in Christ Jesus, we are no longer sinners. We have been made righteous!

2 Corinthians 5:17 Therefore, if anyone is in Christ, he is a new creation; old things have passed away; behold, all things have become new.

No longer do we need to live under guilt and condemnation. We have been made righteous!

We should no longer be sin-conscious. We should be righteousness-conscious.

We should no longer allow Satan to put us down and defeat us.

We know that "we are the righteousness of God in Jesus Christ." We are free from guilt and condemnation.

Romans 8:1 There is therefore now no condemnation to those who are in Christ Jesus, who do not walk according to the flesh, but according to the Spirit.

We are new creatures in Christ Jesus! Our spirits are as righteous as God is Righteous. On a daily basis, our souls and our bodies are being conformed to the image of His Son!

QUESTIONS TO ANSWER

1. According to John 5:24-27, by what authority did Jesus minister when He was on this earth?

2. Describe the work of Jesus as our substitute Redeemer.

3. How is it possible for us to become "the righteousness of God" in Christ?

Lesson Four

The New Creation Image

IN CHRIST

According to apostle Paul, when we accept Jesus as our Savior, we are in Christ. We are new creations. All things become new in our lives.

2 Corinthians 5:17 Therefore, if anyone is in Christ, he is a new creation; old things have passed away; behold, all things have become new.

The moment we accept Jesus as our Savior, the Holy Spirit joins us to Jesus Christ. We become one with Him for all eternity.

Old Things Passed Away

When we become "in Christ," old things pass away. That means parts of us which existed before, no longer exist. Those parts spoken of as the "old things" die. At the same time, there is rebirth – a new spirit person is born.

All Things Become New

A new believer is no longer the person he or she used to be. That person no longer exists. That person has passed away. All things have become new.

How surprising it would be if when we were showing off a new born baby, someone asked, "But what about this baby's past?"

You would answer, "This baby has just been born. He has no past!"

It is the same when the devil comes to remind us of our past failures and sins before we were born again. That part of our old life has passed away. It no longer exists! As new creations, we have no past for the devil to bring accusations against. Paul wrote, "Old things have passed away! All things have become new!"

Born Again

When Jesus talked to Nicodemus, He said you must be born again.

John 3:7 Do not marvel that I said to you, "You must be born again."

At first, Nicodemus thought Jesus was talking about the need for his body to be born again. Then, Jesus made it clear that the part of mankind which was to experience the new birth was not the body or the soul. It was the human spirit.

John 3:5,6 Jesus answered, "Most assuredly, I say to you, unless one is born of water and the Spirit, he cannot enter the kingdom of God. That which is born of the flesh is flesh, and that which is born of the Spirit is spirit."

A New Spirit

At the moment of salvation, our newly created spirit is perfect. It will never become more perfect or righteous than at that moment.

The spirit is the part of us that will live forever. It is the part that is conscious of God's presence. The believer's spirit is the part that can fellowship with God because it is as righteous as God is righteous.

The "stony heart" is gone! God has given us "a heart of flesh." He has given us a heart that is soft, tender, and loving. He has given us a heart that desires to live unto righteousness.

Ezekiel 11:19 Then I will give them one heart, and I will put a new spirit within them, and take the stony heart out of their flesh, and give them a heart of flesh.

Our spirits are perfect in Jesus. God wants to restore our souls through the renewing of the mind. God wants to restore our bodies to perfect health. At the instant of salvation, we became a new creation. The body (bone, flesh, and blood) and soul (intellect, will, and emotion) weren't completely changed, but the spirit became new and perfect at the moment of salvation.

Paul wrote some interesting words to the Philippians - "Work out your own salvation."

Philippians 2:12 Therefore, my beloved, as you have always obeyed, not as in my presence only, but now much more in my absence, work out your own salvation with fear and trembling.

We know that salvation is free; and this verse seems to conflict with others until we understand that at the moment of salvation, our spirits are made perfect in Christ. From that time on, our spirits are working with the Holy Spirit to conform our minds and bodies to the image of Christ. They are being changed daily. Our salvation is working out through our minds and our bodies.

Soul - Finances - Health

Paul continued,

Philippians 2:13 For it is God who works in you both to will and to do for His good pleasure.

It is important that we have a revelation of who our spirit person really is in Christ Jesus. We must understand that our recreated spirit is perfect and absolutely righteous in God's eyes.

With this revelation and with an understanding of the redemptive work of Jesus on our behalf, we will begin to walk in health in our souls and bodies.

Our souls will prosper as our minds are renewed by reading, hearing, meditating, believing, speaking, and acting on the Word of God.

Romans 12:2 And do not be conformed to this world, but be transformed by the renewing of your mind, that you may prove what is that good and acceptable and perfect will of God.

As our souls are transformed - conformed to His image - we will prosper, and our bodies will be in health. John wrote about this.

3 John 1:2 Beloved, I pray that you may prosper in all things and be in health, just as your soul prospers.

RIGHTEOUSNESS OF GOD

How righteous is God?

> ➤ *He is absolute righteousness in His being and in all of His ways.*

> ➤ *His righteousness is more than the absence of sin or the ability not to sin.*

> ➤ *It is an absolute and infinite goodness that can not look upon sin or coexist with sin.*

> ➤ *God is without the ability to sin.*

God in righteousness couldn't overlook the sin of Adam and Eve and their descendants, even though in His love, He would want to.

Romans 3:25,26 Whom God set forth to be a propitiation by His blood, through faith, to demonstrate His righteousness, because in His forbearance God had passed over the sins that were previously committed, to demonstrate at the present time His righteousness, that He might be just and the justifier of the one who has faith in Jesus.

The righteousness of God is revealed by faith.

Romans 1:17 For in it the righteousness of God is revealed from faith to faith; as it is written, "The just shall live by faith."

Our Righteousness

We cannot be made righteous by our own works. The prophet Isaiah painted a clear picture of our righteousness.

Isaiah 64:6a But we are all like an unclean thing, and all our righteousnesses are like filthy rags.

Anything we could do, as hard as we could try, would still be as filthy rags in God's eyes. All of the good things that we did before becoming a new creation added up to a pile of filthy rags.

Imputed Righteousness

When Jesus died on the cross, He took all our sins – our unrighteousness on Himself. He gave us His righteousness in exchange. What a wonderful exchange!

> *Our sin is imputed to Him.*
> *His absolute righteousness is imputed to us.*

The moment we placed our faith in Jesus Christ as our Savior, our spirits became "the righteousness of God."

Romans 3:22 ... even the righteousness of God which is through faith in Jesus Christ to all and on all who believe.

The word "believe" means to trust in, adhere to, and rely on Jesus' redemptive work on our behalf.

Paul stated that when we were re-born and became a new creation, we became the righteousness of God in Jesus.

2 Corinthians 5:21 For He made Him who knew no sin to be sin for us, that we might become the righteousness of God in Him.

When we become the righteousness of God, it doesn't mean only that we are no longer sinners. It doesn't mean only that all of our sins are forgiven - as wonderful as that is. When we become the righteousness of God, it means our spirits are as righteous as God Himself is righteous.

> *We are declared righteous.*
> *We have received God's righteousness.*

Old Unrighteous Image

That we are as righteous as God is righteous, is hard for some to accept. We have been taught so differently by well-meaning teachers.

Many Christians live their whole lives beat down with guilt and condemnation, not knowing who they are in Christ Jesus.

By faith we must accept and believe that we are the righteousness of God. As we become more God-conscious, we become righteousness-conscious instead of sin-conscious.

> ➤ *No Longer a Sinner*

We should no longer look at ourselves as "sinners saved by grace." We are no longer sinners! We are new creations!

Many Christians find themselves sinning because they have been continuously told they are sinners.

They have heard teaching after teaching about sin. Their thoughts have continually dwelt on sin. They haven't received a revelation of righteousness, so sin still rules in their lives. Through the revelation of God's righteousness, we become righteousness-conscious. We see ourselves as God sees us. We see ourselves as righteous as God is righteous. Therefore, sin no longer rules in our bodies. We no longer habitually practice sin.

We see sin as God sees sin. It has lost its attraction because we have had a revelation of God's righteousness.

BEING CONFORMED TO HIS IMAGE

As we continue to walk with a revelation of God's righteousness as new creations in Christ Jesus, we are being transformed by the renewing of our minds. It is a process. We are being conformed daily to the image of His Son.

Romans 8:29 For whom He foreknew, He also predestined to be conformed to the image of His Son, that He might be the firstborn among many brethren.

Confess Sins

If we as believers do commit a sinful act, we don't have to live in defeat, guilt, and condemnation the rest of our lives.

The instant we realize that we have sinned, we must confess that sin to God, and by faith, receive His forgiveness. Then we can keep on walking in righteousness, free from guilt and condemnation.

1 John 1:9 If we confess our sins, He is faithful and just to forgive us our sins and to cleanse us from all unrighteousness.

To confess means to agree with God about our sin. We, like God, must hate sin. The closer we are to God, the more we walk with a revelation of righteousness, the less we will be tempted to sin.

Learn to Rebound

When we fail in some area of our lives, we must learn to be quick to rebound. Like a boxer who has been knocked down on the mat, we are not to lie there feeling sorry for ourselves. Instead, we must train ourselves to bounce off of the mat and jump back to our feet. We are to rebound and keep moving.

When we have sinned, we mustn't give in to thoughts of guilt, condemnation, and defeat. Instead, we must instantly confess our sins and receive that full assurance of God's forgiveness. Like a winning boxer, we must rebound and keep moving toward the victory.

Be Transformed

Our spirits have the righteousness of God, but we are to present our bodies as a living sacrifice to God every day.

Romans 12:1 I beseech you therefore, brethren, by the mercies of God, that you present your bodies a living sacrifice, holy, acceptable to God, which is your reasonable service.

Our spirits have the righteousness of God, but our souls are to be transformed by the renewing of the mind through the revelation of God's Word.

Romans 12:2 And do not be conformed to this world, but be transformed by the renewing of your mind, that you may prove what is that good and acceptable and perfect will of God.

Be Bold

By the revelation of the righteousness of God in the new creation, we can approach the throne of God boldly. We can know that God will hear us.

Hebrews 4:16 Let us therefore come boldly to the throne of grace, that we may obtain mercy and find grace to help in time of need.

We can boldly and confidently come to God because we understand His grace. We know what Jesus has done on our behalf. We know that we have been forgiven. We know that we are new creations in Jesus Christ. We know that we are the righteousness of God.

Be Alive

As new creatures, we have a new life on the inside of us. This new life is the very life of Christ Himself.

Ephesians 2:4,5a But God, who is rich in mercy, because of His great love with which He loved us, even when we were dead in trespasses, made us alive together with Christ ...

The old self that walked according to the course of this world no longer exists. The new inner person has been made alive.

Ephesians 2:1-3 And you He made alive, who were dead in trespasses and sins, in which you once walked according to the course of this world, according to the prince of the power of the air, the spirit who now works in the sons of disobedience, among whom also we all once conducted ourselves in the lusts of our flesh, fulfilling the desires of the flesh and of the mind, and were by nature children of wrath, just as the others.

Be Filled

As new creations, our spirits are filled with the fullness of God. All that He is – has filled us. The richest measure of all that He is has become ours.

Ephesians 3:19 To know the love of Christ which passes knowledge; that you may be filled with all the fullness of God.

The Amplified Bible says,
... that you may be filled (through all your being) unto all the fullness of God – [that is] may have the richest measure of the divine Presence, and become a body wholly filled and flooded with God Himself!

As new creations, we are no longer empty. Instead, we are full of God! We are flooded with His fullness!

As we continue to hunger and thirst after God's righteousness, we will find ourselves filled with the righteousness of God even in our souls and bodies.

Matthew 5:6 Blessed are those who hunger and thirst for righteousness, for they shall be filled.

Receive His Love

What a great revelation it is to know that God isn't mad at us! He loves us! Even while we were His enemies, He loved us.

John 15:12,13,14 This is My commandment, that you love one another as I have loved you. Greater love has no one than this, than to lay down one's life for his friends. You are My friends if you do whatever I command you.

As new creations with a new heart of flesh, we are quick to do what He commands us to do.

➤ *Be Friends with God*

How great it is to know that God isn't mad at us. He is now saying to us, "You are My friends!" We, who were once His enemies, have been reconciled to Him through Christ. We are now His friends and He is our Friend. As friends of God, we have a ministry of reconciliation. We want others to meet our Friend, and like us, to become friends of God.

➢ *Be Reconciled to Him*

As new creations we have been reconciled to Him.

2 Corinthians 5:17,18 Therefore, if anyone is in Christ, he is a new creation; old things have passed away; behold, all things have become new. Now all things are of God, who has reconciled us to Himself through Jesus Christ, and has given us the ministry of reconciliation.

QUESTIONS TO ANSWER

1. What does it mean to be a new creation?

2. Describe the righteousness of God.

3. Describe the righteousness of the new creation.

Lesson Five

Exchanging Our Old Self-Image

The Choice Is Ours

As we study this series of lessons, we are going to come to places where we must make a choice. Will we believe the revelation of God's Word, or will we cling to traditional teachings that we have received over the years?

Will we agree with the apostle Paul when he wrote, **2 Corinthians 5:17 If anyone is in Christ, he is a new creation; old things have passed away; behold, all things have become new?**

We have studied about who we were created to be, about our loving, heavenly Father, and about the great substitutionary, redemptive work of Jesus Christ on our behalf. Now it's time to make a conscious decision to move into all that God has for us.

Putting off Old Self-Image

It's important to have a good self-image. We mustn't let the devil convince us we are unworthy to receive God's blessings. If we do, we will go through life defeated. If we live defeated lives, we will not be able to successfully battle demonic forces. We will not be able to live victorious Christian lives and minister effectively to others.

For many of us, there needs to be a time of deliberately taking off the old man – the habits of the past – and putting on the new creation image by the renewing of our minds.

Paul wrote about putting off the old man. It is an act of our will.

Ephesians 4:22,23 That you put off, concerning your former conduct, the old man which grows corrupt according to the deceitful lusts, and be renewed in the spirit of your mind.

Putting on the New

As we put off the old man, we must be renewed in our minds. This renewing can only come as our minds are renewed to faith by the revelation of God's Word.

Paul went on to say in the next verse.
Ephesians 4:24 And that you put on the new man which was created according to God, in righteousness and true holiness.

As we put off the old man, the old person, the old self-image, and renew our minds to the revelation of God's Word, we are putting on the new person, the new creation.

The new creation is no longer limited to that which he or she perceives by the five senses. The new creation lives in the realm of faith. The new creation knows that he or she is a new creation, created according to God, in righteousness and holiness.

New creation beings no longer see themselves as sinners. They know that their spirits are as righteous and holy as God. They know their souls and bodies are being conformed to the image of the Son into experiential and practical righteousness and holiness in their daily walk.

OLD STRONGHOLDS

As we were growing up, Satan established various strongholds over our minds. Now, even as adults, we think we can't do a particular thing because we were told we couldn't as a child. Damaging words spoken over a period of time have become strong holds that need to be broken.

Inadequacies

Perhaps you were told, "Oh, don't try to do that; your older brother can take care of it." You began to think, "I'm not as capable as my brother."

Inferiority

A teacher may have said, "I don't understand why this is such a problem to you, the rest of the class isn't having trouble with it." Your immediate thought was "I'm not as smart as the rest of the class."

Stereotypes

Perhaps we have believed what others have said about our ethnic background or about a certain group of people that we identify with. These generalities may have become limiting stereotypes over our lives.

If you have red hair, perhaps you have heard, "Redheads always have hot tempers."

Another stereotype might be, "My mother always worried, so this is just the way I am."

We may have heard and believed many things about our race or ethnic background that has made us believe that we don't measure up or favorably compare with others around us. "The Irish always ...," or "The Germans always ..."

The revelation of the new creation will set us free from thoughts of inferiority or inadequacy that may have cast a shadow on our lives in the past.

Prejudice

The revelation of the new creation will set us free from racial prejudice. We will begin to see fellow believers of every race as new creations in Christ.

In the verse immediately preceding Paul's revelation of the new creation, he wrote,

2 Corinthians 5:16a Therefore, from now on, we regard no one according to the flesh.

Paul also wrote to the Galatians,
Galatians 3:26-28 For you are all sons of God through faith in Christ Jesus. For as many of you as were baptized into Christ have put on Christ. There is neither Jew nor Greek, there is neither slave nor free, there is neither male nor female; for you are all one in Christ Jesus.

When we accept Jesus as our personal Savior, we are born again into a new family, the family of God. We must not allow the strongholds of prejudice to remain in our lives. We must see every believer as a new creation and every unbeliever as a potential new creation.

We must see ourselves and all other believers as God sees us. As recreated spirit beings, we are no longer of our former race or ethnic group. We have been born into a new family, the family of God. We no longer will regard another person according to the color of his flesh. We will accept ourselves and others, as new creations in Jesus Christ.

PULLING DOWN STRONGHOLDS

Satan would like to use the old feelings of inferiorities, unworthiness, and prejudices to hold us in bondage. Now is the time to destroy these strongholds.

Destroy Them

If God has revealed strongholds over your mind during this study, you can break them right now. Just say out loud,

> *Satan, I bind you in the name of Jesus. I reject this stronghold of _____(name it)_____ now, in the name of Jesus. I will not allow it to remain any longer. I cast down any thoughts and imaginations that have been contrary to the revelation from God's Word about who I am, what*

I can do or what I can have as a new creation in Jesus Christ!

It may take time to break the habit of thinking or saying the old negative thoughts. However, each time these thoughts come into our minds, we must immediately reject them, cast them down, and continue to declare what the Word of God reveals about the new creation. By so doing, the habit will soon be broken and you will be free. Begin to think and say,

> *The Word of God says I'm a new creation. I'm of the family of God and there is no _____ in God's family. Old things have passed away. I'm a new person in Christ!*

Break the Curses

Satan may have been successful in putting a curse on a family through sin in the past generations. For example, when a person commits suicide, the spirit of suicide stays with that family until it's broken through the power of the name of Jesus.

When a person commits murder, there are spirits of murder that plague the family generation after generation.

There are generational curses or a spirit of inheritance that often opens the door for certain diseases to attach themselves to our bodies. "Oh, yes, heart trouble runs in our family." Or "All the women in our family seem to get cancer."

A generational curse is just as easy to break as a stronghold over our mind. Say,

> *Satan, I bind you in the name of Jesus! I break the curse of _____ and _____! I command all generational curses or any evil spirits of inheritance to be broken over my life right now.*
> *I'm a new creation! I'm a child of God!*
> *I'm now a part of a new family! I'm part of the family of God and there is no bondage, curses, or sickness in God's family!*

When thoughts or symptoms of that bondage, curse, or sickness try to come to you, rebuke them! If you have already been accepting the symptoms, rebuke them immediately and begin to boldly declare what God's Word says about your freedom.

CHANGING THE OLD SELF-IMAGE

To continue to hold a poor image of ourselves is sin. We do not want to be like those the apostle Paul described.

Romans 1:21,22 Although they knew God, they did not glorify Him as God, nor were thankful, but became futile in their thoughts, and their foolish hearts were darkened. Professing to be wise, they became fools.

We are what God says we are. Since Jesus died to set us free from these things, to hold on to them is an insult to God.

Inferiority Complex

Many believers have insecurities about their abilities. They are suffering from a paralyzing fear of failure. God's Word says,

Philippians 4:13 I can do all things through Christ who strengthens me.

2 Timothy 1:7 For God has not given us a spirit of fear, but of power and of love and of a sound mind.

We need to declare continuously,

> *I can do all things through Christ who strengthens me. I know God has given me a spirit of power, of love and of a sound mind.*

Outward Appearance

Many feel insecure about their appearance, thinking or even saying, "I'm too fat," "I'm too skinny," "I wish my hair was a different color," "I wish it wasn't so straight." They are embarrassed or self-conscious about their appearance.

Surveys have revealed that almost all beautiful models and movie stars feel that there's something they would like to change about their appearance.

In our society, there is a tremendous emphasis on outward appearances. But God's Word reveals that we are Spirit-beings created in God's image. We were created to look just like God. Our beauty is in the inward person of the heart – the real person – our spirit on the inside. We can lift up our heads and let the beauty and radiance of Jesus shine from our faces.

When the prophet Samuel came to Bethlehem to anoint one of the sons of Jesse to be the next King, he couldn't help but notice how handsome the oldest son was. Positions of honor normally went to the eldest son, and his immediate thought was that he would probably be the one that God had chosen to be the King. But the Lord stopped him.

1 Samuel 16:7 But the Lord said to Samuel, "Do not look at his appearance or at the height of his stature, because I have refused him. For the Lord does not see as man sees; for man looks at the outward appearance, but the Lord looks at the heart."

Lack of Education

Others feel insecure about their lack of education; however, God's Word reveals that in Christ, we have all the treasures of wisdom and knowledge. Real knowledge is knowing God.

Colossians 2:2,3 ... that their hearts may be encouraged, being knit together in love, and attaining to all riches of the full assurance of understanding, to the knowledge of the mystery of God, both of the Father and of Christ, in whom are hidden all the treasures of wisdom and knowledge.

Feelings of Rejection

Why is it that we see so many believers today that are suffering with rejection, and feelings of rejection, with deep emotional scars in their soul?

God said,
Ephesians 1:5-7 ... having predestined us to adoption as sons by Jesus Christ to Himself, according to the good pleasure of His will, to the praise of the glory of His grace, by which He has made us accepted in the Beloved. In Him we have redemption through His blood, the forgiveness of sins, according to the riches of His grace.

If "we are accepted in the Beloved," then we should not allow feelings of rejection to come against us. We should be secure in the knowledge of our acceptance in Jesus Christ.

The Father God accepts us with the same amount of love as He accepts His own Son, Jesus. We must cast down thoughts of rejection and meditate on the Word until we have a full realization and assurance of our acceptance. Because God accepts us, we can accept ourselves.

False Humility

Often there's a spiritual pride that has developed over years which has mistakenly been called humility.

We sing songs with words like "I'm a poor lost sinner saved by grace." That's not true. Once we are saved we are no longer "poor lost sinners"!

For years we sang the words of a famous old hymn which had the phrase "for such a worm as I." This isn't the way God sees us! This is contrary to the Word of God. We are not poor worms of the dust. We are new creations! We are in Christ! We are being conformed to His image.

An unworthy self-image can be just as defeating in our lives as pride.

Thinking about how unworthy we are may seem to be an expression of humility, but it builds strongholds of defeat over our lives which keep us from realizing our full potential in Jesus Christ.

True Humility

True humility comes from a recognition of God's grace. Humility is a recognition that in past days, while we were enemies of God, undeserving of His great love, He redeemed us so that we could become all that He created us to be.

True humility is thinking good about God. It is knowing that all that we are and all that we can do is because of His great grace and mercy toward us.

It is true that we are not to "think more highly of ourselves than we ought," but neither are we to think lower of ourselves than we should.

If we are to see ourselves being like Jesus and doing the works of Jesus, we must first cast down our old unworthy, "can't-do" images and replace them with images of the new creation.

CHANGING THE SLAVE IMAGE

Many have a slave image of themselves. They see themselves living in the abject poverty of a slave. They haven't been able to picture themselves receiving the blessing and prosperity of God. They haven't seen themselves as children of the King.

Example of Israelites

In Egypt, the children of Israel had known nothing but slavery for hundreds of years. As newly redeemed sons and daughters of God, they needed a revelation of who they were as God's covenant people.

➤ *Gold, Silver*

God wanted to change their self-image from one of the poverty of a slave to a new creation image of redeemed children of God. He instructed them to ask the Egyptians for gold and silver jewelry and expensive ornate clothing.

They were not to put the gold and silver jewelry away in boxes. They were not to put the beautiful articles of clothing away for safe keeping as they traveled through the desert. God told them to put the silver, gold, and the clothing on their sons and daughters.

Exodus 3:21,22a And I will give this people favor in the sight of the Egyptians; and it shall be, when you go, that you shall not go empty-handed. But every woman shall ask of her neighbor, namely, of her who dwells near her house, articles of silver, articles of gold, and clothing; and you shall put them on your sons and on your daughters.

The sons and daughters of Israel – God's chosen people – didn't come out of Egypt in the rags of slavery. The garments and shoes, which didn't wear out on their journey to the promised land, were the garments and jewelry of great wealth.

God was changing their old self-image. He was breaking their old slave-image of themselves.

➢ *To Excess*

Later, when it came time to build the tabernacle, there was so much gold and silver in the possession of the children of Israel that they gave too much. The craftsmen asked Moses to restrain them from giving any more.

Exodus 36:5-7 And they spoke to Moses, saying, "The people bring much more than enough for the service of the work which the LORD commanded us to do."

So Moses gave a commandment, and they caused it to be proclaimed throughout the camp, saying, "Let neither man nor woman do any more work for the offering of the sanctuary." And the people were restrained from bringing, for the material they had was sufficient for all the work to be done—indeed too much.

In the same way God changed the Israelites' image of themselves, He wants to change our old self-image of poverty and slavery to sin. He wants us to experience the joys of our salvation.

CASTING DOWN IMAGINATIONS

How can we get rid of the old self-image which is so displeasing to God?

How can we get rid of the bondage of inferiorities, insecurities, feelings of inadequacy, guilt, condemnation, and unworthiness?

How can we deal with these defeating thoughts and imaginations in our lives?

God's Word gives us the answer.

2 Corinthians 10:5 (KJV) Casting down imaginations, and every high thing that exalteth itself against the knowledge of God, and bringing into captivity every thought to the obedience of Christ.

Imaginations are in the mind. We are to control our minds and cast down every thought that is contrary to the Word of God

The battle is in our minds – in our souls, our wills, our emotions. It's in this area that the battle will be won or lost. Our mind must be renewed with the Word of God.

We are to bring into captivity every thought and make it obedient to Christ. We are to take control and make our thoughts obedient to the knowledge of who we are in Christ.

Like a Snake

If a poisonous snake had fallen from a tree and wrapped itself around our arm, we wouldn't just stand there and look as it prepared to sink its venomous fangs into our skin. No! We would immediately sling our arm down as fast and as hard as we could. It would be an immediate, decisive, forceful action. We would cast down that snake before it could strike.

In the same way, we must, with just as much abhorrence, cast down the thoughts and imaginations of the old self-image. We must shout, "I reject that thought in the name of Jesus!"

> *When our old mind says, "You can't do that you're too shy."*
> *We say "I reject that thought in the name of Jesus. I can do all things through Christ who strengthens me."*
> *When our old mind says, "You have cancer."*
> *We say, "I reject that thought in the name of Jesus. The Word of God says, No plague shall come near my dwelling. I know that by the stripes of Jesus I am healed."*

Mighty Weapons

We have mighty weapons to break the strongholds over our lives.

The apostle Paul wrote,
2 Corinthians 10:4a For the weapons of our warfare are not carnal but mighty in God ...

As we cast down and reject the thoughts and imaginations that are contrary to the knowledge of God, we demolish their power over us.

TAKE OFF THE OLD SELF

The process of taking off our old self is described by the apostle Paul in the book of Colossians.

Colossians 3:9,10 Do not lie to one another, since you have put off the old man with his deeds, and have put on the new man who is renewed in knowledge according to the image of Him who created him.

After we have, by the revelation of God's Word, "put off the old man," we are to "put on the new man," which is being renewed in knowledge to the image of its Creator.

Renewing our Minds

We cannot change how our souls operate by a simple act of our will at the moment of salvation. That is only the first step. We are renewing our minds and being conformed and changed into the image of our Creator as we meditate on the Scripture.

Romans 12:2 And do not be conformed to this world, but be transformed by the renewing of your mind, that you may prove what is that good and acceptable and perfect will of God.

Paul wrote that man is the image and glory of God.

2 Corinthians 3:18 But we all, with unveiled face, beholding as in a mirror the glory of the Lord, are being transformed into the same image from glory to glory, just as by the Spirit of the Lord.

If we were created in God's image, and as a new creation have been restored to God's image, then it's an insult to God to go on saying negative things about ourselves.

We mustn't speak about ourselves as we have in the past. We are new creations. We are being transformed from glory to glory.

CASTING DOWN A GRASSHOPPER IMAGE

A "Can-Do" Image

If we are to live a victorious, successful, Christian life, we need to replace our "can't do" image with a "can do" image. We need to understand that we can do what God's Word says we can do.

Example of Twelve Spies

God promised to give the land of Canaan to the Israelites. The day came when the Lord said to send in one man from each of the twelve tribes to explore the land and to bring back a report. At the end of forty days, they returned with their report.

Numbers 13:27,28a,30-33 Then they told him, and said: "We went to the land where you sent us. It truly flows with milk and honey, and this is its fruit.

"Nevertheless the people who dwell in the land are strong; the cities are fortified and very large."

We Are Able

Then Caleb quieted the people before Moses, and said, "Let us go up at once and take possession, for we are well able to overcome it."

We Are Not Able

But the men who had gone up with him said, "We are not able to go up against the people, for they are stronger than we." And they gave the children of Israel a bad report of the land which they had spied out, saying, "The land through which we have gone as spies is a land that devours its inhabitants, and all the people whom we saw in it are men of great stature.

"There we saw the giants (the descendants of Anak came from the giants); and we were like grasshoppers in our own sight, and so we were in their sight."

Difference Is God

Caleb and Joshua had a true revelation of who God was. They spoke like new creation people should speak. They said, "Let us go up at once and take possession, for we are well able to overcome it."

They continued,
Numbers 14:8,9 If the Lord delights in us, then He will bring us into this land and give it to us, `a land which flows with milk and honey.'

Only do not rebel against the Lord, nor fear the people of the land, for they are our bread; their protection has departed from them, and the Lord is with us. Do not fear them.

The other ten men had seen the same circumstances as Caleb and Joshua. They, however, did not have their eyes on the greatness of God. They looked at their natural abilities and saw themselves as grasshoppers. They had a "grasshopper image" of themselves.

Our Choice

Today, we need to cast down the grasshopper image of ourselves and replace it with a new creation image. Like Caleb and Joshua, we should place our faith in the greatness of God and begin to say, "We are well able to take our land!"

For many, our old self-image has become a strong barrier keeping us from being, having, and doing all that God has for us as new creation beings.

We should boldly speak to the mountain of circumstances and say, "Be removed and be cast into the sea!"

Matthew 21:21 So Jesus answered and said to them, "Assuredly, I say to you, if you have faith and do not doubt, you will not only do what was done to the fig tree, but also if you say to this mountain, `Be removed and be cast into the sea,' it will be done."

The weapons of our warfare are mighty through God to the pulling down of strongholds. The strongholds of our old self-image will crumble and fall. We will become all that God says that we are. As a new creation, the old self-image will pass away and all things, including our newly discovered self-image, will become new.

2 Corinthians 5:17 Therefore, if anyone is in Christ, he is a new creation; old things have passed away; behold, all things have become new.

QUESTIONS TO ANSWER

1. What are some of the strongholds of the old self-image that you have "cast down" as a result of this study?

2. Describe the process mentioned in Colossians 3:9,10 as putting off the old man and putting on the new man.

3. How can we effectively renew our minds as mentioned in Romans 12:2?

Lesson Six

Our Image In Christ

OUR FAMILY IN CHRIST

The New Birth

The moment we receive Jesus Christ as our personal Savior, we are "born again" into a new family.

Jesus told Nicodemus,
John 3:7 Do not marvel that I said to you, "You must be born again."

Jesus made it clear to Nicodemus that He was not talking about being born of the flesh, but that to be "born again" means to be born of the spirit.

John 3:5,6 Jesus answered, "Most assuredly, I say to you, unless one is born of water and the Spirit, he cannot enter the kingdom of God. That which is born of the flesh is flesh, and that which is born of the Spirit is spirit."

Before accepting Jesus as our Savior, while we were alive in our bodies (bone, flesh and blood) and our souls (intellect, emotions and wills), we were dead spiritually. At the moment of salvation we were "born again" spiritually. Our spirits became alive. We became new creations in Jesus Christ.

We were born into a new family, the family of God. When we were born into God's family, we became His children.

Children of God

The apostle John wrote,
1 John 3:1a Behold what manner of love the Father has bestowed on us, that we should be called children of God!

If we understand we are the sons and daughters of the most powerful, most intelligent, wisest Father in the universe, we can't help but realize that our lives, positions, rights, benefits, and futures, have completely changed.

Understanding our new family relationship as God's sons and daughters can completely change the way we think about ourselves.

Paul wrote,
Romans 8:14 For as many as are led by the Spirit of God, these are sons of God.

When we accept Jesus Christ as our Lord and Savior, we become the children of God.

John 1:12 But as many as received Him, to them He gave the right to become children of God, even to those who believe in His name.

The word "right" means legal authority. Once we believe, we have the legal authority to become a son or daughter of God.

Heirs of God

God hasn't only made us His children, He has also given us an inheritance with the same rewards as Jesus. We are joint heirs with Christ.

Romans 8:17a ... and if children, then heir–heirs of God and joint heirs with Christ ...

The wealth and possessions of the Father are beyond measure, and all that the Father has belongs to His Son.

How overwhelming it is to realize that we, having been born into God's family, have become joint heirs with Jesus Christ. All of His inheritance has become our inheritance.

All of the riches of heaven belong to Jesus, and because we are joint heirs with Him, all of the riches of heaven also belong to us.

Ephesians 1:3 Blessed be the God and Father of our Lord Jesus Christ, who has blessed us with every spiritual blessing in the heavenly places in Christ.

Possessing Our Inheritance

By faith in Jesus, we are born into the family of God, and become sons and daughters of God. As children of God, we receive a promised inheritance.

Galatians 3:26 For you are all sons of God through faith in Christ Jesus.

Ezekiel 46:16 Thus says the Lord God: "If the prince gives a gift of some of his inheritance to any of his sons, it shall belong to his sons; it is their possession by inheritance."

As new creations, we must possess our possessions. We must possess what is rightfully ours by inheritance.

Receiving Our Benefits

How wonderful it is to know about our benefits as sons and daughters of our Heavenly Father. How exciting it is to realize that we don't have to wait until we get to heaven to start enjoying our inheritance.

The apostle Paul wrote,
Philippians 4:19 And my God shall supply all your need according to His riches in glory by Christ Jesus.

We can start enjoying our inheritance now as new creations, having already been "born again" into the family of God.

As new creations, children of God, and joint heirs with Jesus Christ, we don't have to cry and beg God to supply our needs on this earth. All that God has is already ours. All we need to do is find out how to receive God's riches by faith and obedience.

> ➤ *Power to Get Wealth*

Moses spoke these words to the children of Israel,
Deuteronomy 8:18 And you shall remember the LORD your God, for it is He who gives you power to get wealth, that He may establish His covenant which He swore to your fathers, as it is this day.

> ➤ *A Nature to Give*

It is the Father's nature to give.

John wrote,
John 3:16a For God so loved the world that He gave ...

Because we are our Father's children, it should be in our new nature to be givers.

Jesus said,
Luke 6:38 Give, and it will be given to you: good measure, pressed down, shaken together, and running over will be put into your bosom. For with the same measure that you use, it will be measured back to you.

> ➤ *A Storehouse of Blessings*

As we give to God in faith and obedience, we are handing God a measure to use in blessing us. Thereby all our needs are met out of the great storehouse of our eternal inheritance.

In the book of Malachi we read,
**Malachi 3:10 "Bring all the tithes into the storehouse, that there may be food in My house, and prove Me now in this,"
says the LORD of hosts, "If I will not open for you the windows of heaven and pour out for you such blessing that there will not be room enough to receive it."**

How wonderful it is to know how to receive our blessings as new creation sons and daughters of God.

THE BODY OF CHRIST

As new creations, we not only became part of the family of God, but by the miracle of the new birth, we became part of the body of Christ.

The apostle Paul wrote,
1 Corinthians 12:27 Now you are the body of Christ, and members individually.

All believers, collectively, make up the body of Christ. We, individually, are members of that body.

We Are Important Part

God has a place for every believer in His body. He has a definite function for us to fulfill.

v. 18 But now God has set the members, each one of them, in the body just as He pleased.

> ➤ *Need One Another*

Every believer in the body of Christ needs the other parts.

vs. 21,22 And the eye cannot say to the hand, "I have no need of you"; nor again the head to the feet, "I have no need of you." No, much rather, those members of the body which seem to be weaker are necessary.

vs. 26 And if one member suffers, all the members suffer with it; or if one member is honored, all the members rejoice with it.

Every part of God's body is important! Just as the human body has the ability to care for, help, and create, so has the body of Christ.

OUR POSITION IN CHRIST

At the moment of salvation, the Holy Spirit baptized us into Jesus Christ. By the miracle of the new birth, we became intimately united with Jesus. We became one with Him.

1 Corinthians 12:13 For by one Spirit we were all baptized into one body—whether Jews or Greeks, whether slaves or free—and have all been made to drink into one Spirit.

The word baptism means:

> ➤ *to be totally identified with*

At the moment of salvation, we became totally identified with Jesus Christ.

When a piece of white cloth is placed in a vat of red dye, the cloth takes on the color of the dye. It becomes identified with the dye as it is "baptized" into it. In the same way, our spirits take on the nature of the Son of God when we are baptized into Him by the Holy Spirit at the moment of salvation. We become totally identified with Him–intimately united with Him–part of His body–one with Him.

> *All that Jesus is, we are!*
> *All that Jesus has is ours!*
> *All that we are and have is because*
> *we are in Him.*

As Taught in Ephesians

Paul mentioned our position and possessions "in Christ" repeatedly in the first three chapters of his letter to the Ephesians.

➤ *Blessed with Spiritual Blessings*

He wrote that we are blessed with every spiritual blessing in Christ.

Ephesians 1:3 Blessed be the God and Father of our Lord Jesus Christ, who has blessed us with every spiritual blessing in the heavenly places in Christ.

All the rich, glorious, and satisfying spiritual blessings of heaven are available for us to receive and enjoy in our daily lives.

➤ *Chosen in Him*

The Father chose Jesus. He is the chosen One. Because we are in Him, we now share in His choosing.

Ephesians 1:4 Just as He chose us in Him before the foundation of the world, that we should be holy and without blame before Him in love.

God did not choose us because of our looks, our abilities, or our self-worth. He chose us because in eternity past, He saw us in Christ.

➤ *Predestined in Him*

We share His destiny because we are in Him.

Ephesians 1:5 Having predestined us to adoption as sons by Jesus Christ to Himself, according to the good pleasure of His will.

We are not predestined to spend eternity with God because He likes us more than He likes others. The Father could look down through the ages and see us in Christ. He chose us because He chose Jesus, and we are one with Him.

Our inheritance and our predestination are because of our position in Jesus Christ.

Ephesians 1:11 In whom also we have obtained an inheritance, being predestined according to the purpose of Him who works all things according to the counsel of His will.

> *Accepted in Him*

We are accepted in the Beloved. Our acceptance by the Father is because we are in Christ.

Ephesians 1:6 To the praise of the glory of His grace, by which He has made us accepted in the Beloved.

Our redemption, forgiveness, and all the riches of His grace are because we are in Him.

Ephesians 1:7 In Him we have redemption through His blood, the forgiveness of sins, according to the riches of His grace.

> *Sealed in Him*

We were sealed by the Holy Spirit as He intimately united, and eternally made us one with Jesus Christ.

Ephesians 1:13 In Him you also trusted, after you heard the word of truth, the gospel of your salvation; in whom also, having believed, you were sealed with the Holy Spirit of promise.

> *Seated with Him*

Because we are one with Him, we are seated together with Him in heavenly places.

Ephesians 2:6 And raised us up together, and made us sit together in the heavenly places in Christ Jesus even though we are living in our bodies on this earth positionally, in Christ we are seated in heaven. When Jesus completed His redemptive work, He sat down at the right hand of the Father.

Psalms 110:1 The Lord said to my Lord, "Sit at My right hand, till I make Your enemies Your footstool."

Paul revealed that we are seated with Him positionally. We are enjoying all of the benefits of His completed work on this earth. We are, by faith, enjoying the moment by moment rest that is available for every believer, even in the midst of the storms of life.

> *Good Works in Him*

We were created in Christ Jesus for good works.

Ephesians 2:10 For we are His workmanship, created in Christ Jesus for good works, which God prepared beforehand that we should walk in them.

Adam and Eve were created for a purpose, and in Christ we are created for the same purpose. We are created to do

His works here on earth. We are the body of Christ operating on earth in His place.

When Jesus was alive and ministering on this earth, He told His believers,

John 14:12 Most assuredly, I say to you, he who believes in Me, the works that I do he will do also; and greater works than these he will do, because I go to My Father.

As believers in Jesus Christ, we are the body of Jesus. We are His legs, His feet, His arms, and His hands on this earth. As the body of Jesus, we are continuing to do His works today.

The body of Christ:

➤ *Represents Christ to the world*

➤ *Brings God's love to the world*

➤ *Brings God's healing and deliverance*

➤ *Brings people to a saving knowledge of God*

➤ *Made Near in Him*

We, who were His enemies and far off from Him, have been "made near" by His blood because we are in Him.

Ephesians 2:13 But now in Christ Jesus you who once were far off have been made near by the blood of Christ.

We can now enjoy a continual, close fellowship and communion with Him.

➤ *Become One*

When we were created in Him, all enmity between us and God was abolished. The two of us suddenly became one.

Ephesians 2:15 Having abolished in His flesh the enmity, that is, the law of commandments contained in ordinances, so as to create in Himself one new man from the two, thus making peace.

The new creation person cannot be separated from Jesus and His peace, as long as he or she remains one with Him.

➤ *A Holy Temple*

In Him, we are being built together as a holy temple, as the dwelling place of God Himself.

Ephesians 2:20-22 Having been built on the foundation of the apostles and prophets, Jesus Christ Himself being the chief cornerstone, In whom the whole building, being joined together, grows into a holy temple in the Lord, in whom you also are being built together for a habitation of God in the Spirit.

How exciting it is to discover that God has chosen to dwell with us on this earth. He has chosen to live within us individually and to corporately dwell within all of us as His church.

➢ *Boldness - Confidence in Him*

Because we are in Him, one with Him, totally united with Him, as a new creation we share everything that He is and everything that He has.

His righteousness has become our righteousness. His destiny has become our destiny. His life has become our life.

When we receive the revelation of the new creation, we can boldly say,

> *I know who I am in Jesus Christ!*
> *I have become one with Him!*
> *I now share His righteousness,*
> *His destiny, and His life!*
> *I am a new creation!*
> *Old things have passed away!*
> *All things have become new!*

Ephesians 3:12 In whom we have boldness and access with confidence through faith in Him.

We can come boldly into His presence with full confidence that because we are in Him, we are no longer under guilt and condemnation. We are new creations. We are the righteousness of God in Jesus Christ.

Children of Light

Jesus was God manifested in the flesh. Jesus was sent to this spiritually dark world as light to reveal God's love and power to those who would believe on Him.

John 8:12 Then Jesus spoke to them again, saying, "I am the light of the world. He who follows Me shall not walk in darkness, but have the light of life."

1 Thessalonians 5:5 You are all sons of light and sons of the day. We are not of the night nor of darkness.

Believers are to live as children of the light. They are to live victoriously according to the light of the revelation of God's Word. Paul instructs us by saying,

Ephesians 5:8 For you were once darkness, but now you are light in the Lord. Walk as children of light.

Washed, Sanctified, Justified

As new creations, we have been set free from sin. We have been washed, sanctified, and justified.

1 Corinthians 6:10,11 ... **nor thieves, nor covetous, nor drunkards, nor revilers, nor extortioners will inherit the kingdom of God. And such were some of you. But you were washed, but you were sanctified, but you were justified in the name of the Lord Jesus and by the Spirit of our God.**

To be washed, is to be made clean. God cannot allow uncleanness in His presence. Perfect justice and perfect righteousness cannot abide with sin.

1 John 1:7 But if we walk in the light as He is in the light, we have fellowship with one another, and the blood of Jesus Christ His Son cleanses us from all sin.

"Sanctified" describes the relationship men can have with God through faith in Christ. It means we are set apart from evil, and set apart unto Christ. We are set apart from the world, and have a relationship with God based on His righteousness imputed to us.

We are washed and sanctified. We are also justified. To be justified means to be judicially declared righteous by God. We are righteous; our spirits are perfect before God. In Christ we are new creations. The old sins are gone – washed away through the shed blood of Jesus.

Romans 3:28 Therefore we conclude that a man is justified by faith apart from the deeds of the law.

Romans 8:31b,33 If God is for us, who can be against us?

Who shall bring a charge against God's elect? It is God who justifies.

When Satan and his crowd come to remind us of the past, we should say,

> *Forget it, Satan,*
> *I've been washed, sanctified, and justified!*
> *I'm a new creation!*
> *Old things have passed away!*
> *All things have become new!*

OUR NEW CITIZENSHIP

Our Rights

As a new creation, we have a new citizenship.

A citizen of a country is guaranteed certain inalienable rights under the constitution of the nation. The constitution is the supreme law of the land. All other laws of the nation are subject to the basic rights given by the constitution. If we don't know what our rights are, we can be deprived of them by some unscrupulous person.

As new creations, we have been given many inalienable rights, but we can be deprived of our rights by an unscrupulous Satan. We can be made to suffer needlessly. Being a new creation doesn't guarantee that we will enjoy all our spiritual blessings, but it does give us the legal right to reclaim them.

Our Weapons

In this world, Satan has usurped our rights as new creations. However, God has given us the spiritual weapons we need to reclaim them.

Paul wrote that our weapons aren't of this world, and that they have divine power, strong enough to pull down strongholds.

2 Corinthians 10:4 For the weapons of our warfare are not carnal but mighty in God for pulling down strongholds ...

A stronghold is like a fortress. It has a tight grip over situations, over thoughts, persons, or organizations. It may be a stronghold which Satan has established over our health or finances. Whatever the stronghold is, we have the weapons to pull it down!

➢ *To Be Effective*

No weapon is effective unless it's used.

If an enemy were to attack an armed person, he could still harm him if that person didn't use his weapons. The person who is under attack could be armed from head to toe, but unless he used his weapons, he could still be defeated.

The same is true for us as new creation beings. We have at our disposal all the weapons we will ever need to defeat the enemy, but we must learn what they are and how to use them.

➤ *Described*

Paul described the armor and the weapons of the new creation in the book of Ephesians.

Ephesians 6:11-17 Put on the whole armor of God, that you may be able to stand against the wiles of the devil.

For we do not wrestle against flesh and blood, but against principalities, against powers, against the rulers of the darkness of this age, against spiritual hosts of wickedness in the heavenly places.

Therefore take up the whole armor of God, that you may be able to withstand in the evil day, and having done all, to stand.

Stand therefore, having girded your waist with truth, having put on the breastplate of righteousness, and having shod your feet with the preparation of the gospel of peace; above all, taking the shield of faith with which you will be able to quench all the fiery darts of the wicked one. And take the helmet of salvation, and the sword of the Spirit, which is the word of God.

➤ *One Offensive Weapon*

There are two general types of weapons, defensive and offensive. Some weapons are for our defense when we are attacked, and one is for the purpose of attacking the enemy.

The sword of the Spirit – the Word of God – is the offensive weapon mentioned in this descriptive passage. When we speak the Word of God in faith, the devil has to let go. He has no defense against this weapon.

God has given this weapon to us, but we must learn to use it. As new creations, we must speak God's Word to the circumstances which attempt to pull us down.

In Conclusion

We have a new image in Christ.

By the miracle of the new birth, we have been born into the family of God. As sons and daughters of God, we have become co-heirs with Jesus. All that belongs to Him is now ours to share.

We are in Him, and because of our new position, we are blessed with all spiritual blessings, chosen, predestined, accepted, sealed, and seated with Him.

We are created in Christ to do His good works on this earth. We, who were once His enemies, are allowed to have close fellowship with Him. We are His holy temple. We have a fresh new boldness and confidence because of our faith in Him.

We who were once in darkness are now described as children of light. We have been washed, sanctified, and justified. We have citizenship rights as new creations. We must put on the whole armor of God and reclaim all our inheritance, our benefits, and our rights as new creations in Jesus Christ.

QUESTIONS TO ANSWER

1. What does the new birth mean to you?

2. What does it mean to you to be "in Christ?

3. What does it mean to you to be a part of the Children of the Light?

Lesson Seven

New Creation Rights

AS CHILDREN OF ABRAHAM

The apostle Paul wrote that if we are of faith, we are children of Abraham. This is important because as children of Abraham, we have many rights and privileges.

Galatians 3:6,7 ... just as Abraham "believed God, and it was accounted to him for righteousness." Therefore know that only those who are of faith are sons of Abraham.

Righteousness of Abraham

God looked on Abraham as righteous not due to his good works, his exemplary life, or his great worth, but because Abraham had faith. Abraham wasn't perfect, but he was righteous because of his faith.

We don't have to be perfect to have the righteousness of God. However, we must believe God and receive His righteousness by faith, even as Abraham did.

In the physical realm, we are of our earthly father, born into a family which bears his name. When we are born again through faith, we are born into the family of faith and have a right to use the family name – the family of Abraham.

God's Promise to Abraham

When God called Abram (later called Abraham) out of Haran, He gave him many promises; and since we are in Abraham's family, we can share in these promises.

Genesis 12:1-3 Now the Lord had said to Abram: "Get out of your country, from your kindred and from your father's house, to a land that I will show you.

"I will make you a great nation; I will bless you and make your name great; and you shall be a blessing. I will bless those who bless you, and I will curse him who curses you; and in you all the families of the earth shall be blessed."

We are entitled to the blessings of Abraham! We can claim these promises for our own.

His Descendants

God promised Abraham a great number of descendants. His seed was to be as many as the grains of dust in the earth – a reference to his physical seed.

Genesis 13:16 And I will make your descendants as the dust of the earth; so that if a man could number the dust of the earth, then your descendants also could be numbered.

God also told Abraham that his descendants would be as numerous as the stars in the sky – referring to his spiritual seed through faith.

Genesis 15:5 Then He brought him outside and said, "Look now toward heaven, and count the stars if you are able to number them." And He said to him, "So shall your descendants be."

Everlasting Covenant

God established with Abraham and his descendants an everlasting covenant. Through faith, we are his descendants and we are part of this everlasting covenant.

Genesis 17:7 And I will establish My covenant between Me and you and your descendants after you in their generations, for an everlasting covenant, to be God to you and your descendants after you.

Jesus, the Seed of Abraham

If we are in Jesus, we are heirs of the promise of God's blessing to Abraham. We are heirs to the covenant of Abraham.

Galatians 3:16 Now to Abraham and his Seed were the promises made. He does not say, "And to seeds," as of many, but as of one, "And to your Seed," who is Christ.

Galatians 3:29 And if you are Christ's, then you are Abraham's seed, and heirs according to the promise.

OUR BLESSINGS IN ABRAHAM

We are children of Abraham – his spiritual descendants – and by faith we can receive his blessings. If we are to receive these blessings by faith, we must know what they are.

List of Blessings

Deuteronomy 28:1-14 Now it shall come to pass, if you diligently obey the voice of the Lord your God, to observe carefully all His commandments which I command you today, that the Lord your God will set you high above all nations of the earth. And all these blessings shall come upon you and overtake you, because you obey the voice of the Lord your God:

Blessed shall you be in the city, and blessed shall you be in the country. Blessed shall be the fruit of your body, the produce of your ground and the increase of your herds, the increase of your cattle and the offspring of your flocks. Blessed shall be your basket and your kneading bowl. Blessed shall you be when you come in, and blessed shall you be when you go out.

The Lord will cause your enemies who rise against you to be defeated before your face; they shall come out against you one way and flee before you seven ways.

The Lord will command the blessing on you in your storehouses and in all to which you set your hand, and He will bless you in the land which the Lord your God is giving you.

The Lord will establish you as a holy people to Himself, just as He has sworn to you, if you keep the commandments of the Lord your God and walk in His ways. Then all peoples of the earth shall see that you are called by the name of the Lord, and they shall be afraid of you.

And the Lord will grant you plenty of goods, in the fruit of your body, in the increase of your livestock, and in the produce of your ground, in the land of which the Lord swore to your fathers to give you.

The Lord will open to you His good treasure, the heavens, to give the rain to your land in its season, and to bless all the work of your hand. You shall lend to many nations, but you shall not borrow. And the Lord will make you the head and not the tail; you shall be above only, and not be beneath, if you heed the commandments of the Lord your God, which I command you today, and are careful to observe them. So you shall not turn aside from any of the words which I command you this day, to the right hand or to the left, to go after other gods to serve them.

Given to Us

These promises were given first to Abraham, then to his physical descendants, and then they were given to his spiritual descendants – those who are of faith.

Galatians 3:6,7,14 ... just as Abraham "believed God, and it was accounted to him for righteousness." Therefore know that only those who are of faith are sons of Abraham.

... that the blessing of Abraham might come upon the Gentiles in Christ Jesus, that we might receive the promise of the Spirit through faith.

For Today

Notice that the promises given to Abraham are for now, not for when we get to heaven. They are for today.

Let's take time to thank the Lord for some of our new creation blessings.

> *Father,*
> *I thank you that I am blessed in the city and blessed in the country. I am blessed wherever I am.*
> *I thank you that the fruit of my womb is blessed, my children are blessed.*

I thank you Lord that my animals are blessed by you.

I thank you Lord that my basket is full, that I have food for every day.

I thank you Lord that I am blessed as I come in and blessed as I go out. I know that when an enemy tries to come against me, he's already defeated. He will come against me in one direction, but he will flee in seven directions.

Lord, I thank you that everything I do shall prosper. I am going to walk in your ways today, tomorrow, and every day of my life.

I thank you Lord that people will see how great you are through my life.

I thank you Lord that you will give me abundant prosperity.

I thank you Lord that you have opened the storehouse of bounty in heaven, and that I can receive it on earth.

I thank you Lord that you have made me the head and not the tail – you have put me at the top and not the bottom.

Oh Father, I thank you for all your blessings! I will not turn aside from following you, Lord. I will not serve other gods. I will keep your commandments.

In Jesus' Name,
Amen

FREE FROM LAW OF SIN AND DEATH

Saved by Grace

Paul stated that sin no longer has legal control or authority over those who profess Jesus as their Lord and Savior.

We no longer live under the law. We are saved – redeemed – not by the law, but by grace.

Romans 6:14 For sin shall not have dominion over you, for you are not under law but under grace.

Ephesians 2:8 For by grace you have been saved through faith, and that not of yourselves; it is the gift of God.

The definition of grace is unmerited favor – something given to us that we didn't deserve.

Not only did we not deserve God's unmerited favor, we deserved the exact opposite. Men and women couldn't fulfill the law; and so, it couldn't bring them salvation – it could only bring death.

To be saved means to be saved from something or to be delivered from something. What are we delivered from?

Free from Curse

We are no longer under the law of sin and death, and we are no longer under the curse of the law. We have been redeemed from the curse of the law; and yet, if we don't know our rights as new creations, when Satan or his demon spirits come to put curses on us, we can be defeated. However, when we know our new creation rights and privileges, we can win every battle.

When these things come against us which have been revealed as part of the curse, we as new creations can boldly say,

I have been redeemed from the curse of the law.

➤ *Jesus Became Curse*

Jesus became this curse for us! He became our substitute and took these curses on His own body in order to redeem us from them! He freed us from every one of the curses of the law when He paid our penalty on the cross.

Galatians 3:13 Christ has redeemed us from the curse of the law, having become a curse for us (for it is written, "Cursed is everyone who hangs on a tree.")

Jesus was the only one who was ever able to keep the law completely. He lived a perfect life under the law and so became the perfect sacrifice.

➤ *Redeemed from Curse*

It's important to know what's included under the curse. What did Jesus take upon Himself for us? What is the curse of the law? As we study this section, we may discover we have been accepting things from Satan that we don't have to accept.

Moses listed many things that are part of the curse in Deuteronomy 28:15-68. (It would be good to read this entire section). Moses also listed the curses that come as a result of disobedience and the following is a brief summary.

Deuteronomy 28:15,20 But it shall come to pass, if you do not obey the voice of the Lord your God, to observe carefully all His commandments and His statutes which I command you today, that all these curses will come upon you and overtake you:

The Lord will send on you cursing, confusion, and rebuke in all that you set your hand to do, until you are destroyed and until you perish quickly, because of the wickedness of your doings in which you have forsaken Me.

What are the curses of the law? What are the penalties of not keeping the law?

> ➤ *Plagued with diseases*
>
> ➤ *Fever, inflammation*
>
> ➤ *Scorching heat and drought*
>
> ➤ *Blight and mildew*
>
> ➤ *Sky of bronze*
>
> ➤ *Ground of iron*
>
> ➤ *Rain turned to dust and powder*
>
> ➤ *Defeat*
>
> ➤ *Bodies become food for birds and beasts*
>
> ➤ *Boils, tumors, festering sores, itch*
>
> ➤ *Madness, blindness, confusion of mind*
>
> ➤ *Unsuccessful in everything we do, oppressed, robbed*
>
> ➤ *Loss of loved one, house, fruit of labor*
>
> ➤ *Loss of possessions, children*

This is just the beginning of the list!

Practical Application

Now, take time to read the curses of the law from Deuteronomy again, but this time remember that Jesus has redeemed you from the curse of the law and add the words, "Jesus has redeemed me from _____ . For example,

> **Jesus has redeemed me from the plague of diseases.**
> **Jesus has redeemed me from the wasting diseases.**
> **Jesus has redeemed me from fever and inflammation.**
> **Jesus has redeemed me from scorching heat and drought.**
> **Jesus has redeemed me from ...**

Find those things listed in Deuteronomy 28 which Satan has been putting on you. They are part of the curse of the law and Jesus has redeemed you from that particular curse!

Begin to agree with God's Word,

> *I am redeemed by Jesus from the curse of*
> *_____ . Jesus paid my penalty for sin. I*
> *command every symptom of this curse to leave me*
> *now!*

When Jesus was nailed to the cross, He became a curse for us so that we might be made righteous. He not only gave us the gift of eternal life, Jesus gave us everything we need to be victorious in this life.

When Satan tries to bring one of those curses, say,

> *Oh, no you don't Satan! Jesus has redeemed me*
> *from that curse!*

Freedom from Past

Often Satan will entrap us into accepting one of the curses by convincing us that we have sinned, and that this curse is the penalty for that sin. We begin to think we deserve what he's putting on us.

Satan is correct when he tells us the curses come as a result of sin. But Satan never reminds us that Jesus has already paid the penalty for that sin, so that we no longer need to bear that sin or the curse that comes as a result of that sin.

2 Corinthians 5:17 Therefore, if anyone is in Christ, he is a new creation; old things have passed away; behold, all things have become new.

Victorious Living

As new creation beings, we are free from the law of sin and death. We have been redeemed from every sin, every penalty, and every curse.

Romans 8:2 For the law of the Spirit of life in Christ Jesus has made me free from the law of sin and death.

If we do commit sin, we must confess it and receive forgiveness for it.

1 John 1:9 If we confess our sins, He is faithful and just to forgive us our sins and to cleanse us from all unrighteousness.

When we confess our sin, we are immediately freed from the hold that sin has over us. We are cleansed from all unrighteousness. Satan can no longer defeat us through accusations of guilt and condemnation.

Sin, its curse, and the law of sin and death, doesn't have any legal right to bring defeat. We can live with the blessings of the new creation on our lives.

With Power to Overcome

Abraham had faith and it was counted unto him for righteousness. By faith, we can receive the blessings given to him.

Jesus came and took the curse of the law upon Himself. By faith, we receive our salvation. By faith, we can overcome the things of this world. Faith gives us the power to overcome!

1 John 5:4 For whatever is born of God overcomes the world. And this is the victory that has overcome the world—our faith.

As new creations, we possess God's victorious power within us. The choice is left up to us as to whether we allow this power to operate or not. We can choose to believe God's Word, or we can choose to believe the circumstances surrounding us.

The victorious power of God is released when we believe and release His Word by boldly speaking it forth. It's our faith in His Word which gives us the victory.

Satan tells us that we are guilty, worthless sinners, and that we are helpless against the sickness, pain, poverty, and despair which are parts of the curse.

➢ *God says we are new creations, free from guilt, condemnation, and the curse of the law.*

➢ *God says we are heirs of all the promised blessings of Abraham.*

➢ *God says as overcomers, we can walk in His abundant blessings.*

We can be, do, and have all that God has provided for us as believers in Jesus Christ.

➢ *We must choose to believe God instead of the lies of the devil.*

➢ *We must choose to see ourselves as God sees us.*

➢ *We must begin to declare all that God has said about ourselves.*

Then we can enjoy our wonderful rights as new creations in Jesus Christ!

QUESTIONS TO ANSWER

1. Why is it important to understand that we are of the family of Abraham?
2. List some of the covenant promise God made with Abraham that are important to you.
3. Using Deuteronomy 28:15-68, write a page of declarations stating your freedom from the curses of the law.

Lesson Eight

New Creation Benefits

Introduction

The revelation of the new creation and our righteousness in Jesus brings many benefits to the believer in Jesus Christ.

Psalm 68:19a   Blessed be the Lord, Who daily loads us with benefits ...

FELLOWSHIP WITH GOD

One of the greatest benefits of the new creation is that we can walk confidently and unashamedly with God in the light of His glorious presence. We can talk with Him. We can have close and intimate fellowship with Him.

1 John 1:3-7   That which we have seen and heard we declare to you, that you also may have fellowship with us; and truly our fellowship is with the Father and with His Son Jesus Christ. And these things we write to you that your joy may be full.

This is the message which we have heard from Him and declare to you, that God is light and in Him is no darkness at all. If we say that we have fellowship with Him, and walk in darkness, we lie and do not practice the truth. But if we walk in the light as He is in the light, we have fellowship with one another, and the blood of Jesus Christ His Son cleanses us from all sin.

Christianity is different from every other religion in that when we accept Christ, we can have a personal relationship (part of eternal family of God) and fellowship (daily communion) with God.

God's purpose in redemption was to restore His relationship with mankind, and to restore our fellowship with Him.

Definition

According to **Webster's Unabridged Dictionary**, some of the definitions of fellowship are:

➤ *The condition of being an associate*

➤ *Mutual association of persons on equal and friendly terms*

➤ *Communion*

➤ *Companionship*

> ➢ *Intimate familiarity*
> ➢ *A mutual sharing*

A Calling

We are called to fellowship with God.

1 Corinthians 1:9 God is faithful, by whom you were called into the fellowship of His Son, Jesus Christ our Lord.

What an awesome thought. God has called us into fellowship with Himself. God wants to have fellowship with us!

Our intimate fellowship with God should lead to the same level of fellowship with our brothers and sisters in the family of God. The apostle John wrote,

1 John 1:3,4 That which we have seen and heard we declare to you, that you also may have fellowship with us; and truly our fellowship is with the Father and with His Son Jesus Christ. And these things we write to you that your joy may be full.

Brings Joy

Joy is the result of an intimate, unhindered fellowship with God, and with fellow believers in Jesus Christ.

Psalm 16:11 You will show me the path of life; in Your presence is fullness of joy; at Your right hand are pleasures forevermore.

There is no greater joy than that which is experienced by intimate fellowship with God Himself through His Word. Jeremiah wrote,

Jeremiah 15:16 Your words were found, and I ate them, and Your word was to me the joy and rejoicing of my heart; for I am called by Your name, O LORD God of hosts.

The believer, who has found the revelation of being a new creation in Jesus, has found joy.

Once those who were oppressed by thoughts of guilt, condemnation, and unworthiness, discover the revelation of righteousness, they are released from bondage into overwhelming joy and rejoicing.

Only those who have experienced the revelation of the new creation can experience the overwhelming joy of intimate fellowship with God without fear of condemnation.

David wrote about this joy.
Psalms 32:1,2 (TLB) What happiness for those whose guilt has been forgiven! What joys when sins are covered over! What relief for those who have confessed their sins and God has cleared their record.

Broken Fellowship

If we sin, our relationship with God is unbroken. We are still His children.

Through sin, our fellowship with Him is broken. Once again, sin has become a barrier between us and God. However, in His great mercy, God made a provision for our fellowship with Him to be immediately restored.

John wrote,

1 John 1:8-10 If we say that we have no sin, we deceive ourselves, and the truth is not in us. If we confess our sins, He is faithful and just to forgive us our sins and to cleanse us from all unrighteousness. If we say that we have not sinned, we make Him a liar, and His word is not in us.

"Confess" means to name it. We are to name our sin and not deceive ourselves, trying to hide or deny that we have sinned. Instead, we are quickly to admit to ourselves and to God that what we have done is sin in His eyes and in our own eyes.

The word "sin" means to "miss the mark." We sin anytime we miss the mark of God's perfect righteousness by our thoughts or actions.

The moment we recognize that we have "missed the mark," we must immediately confess our sin and receive God's forgiveness and cleansing from that unrighteousness.

➤ *Abusing God's Grace*

Many who do not have a revelation of righteousness, have abused the grace of God. They have mistakenly thought that this means they can willfully sin as long as they confess it later and receive God's forgiveness.

John made it clear, as he continued in the next verse, that we are not to willfully allow sin to come into our lives.

1 John 2:1 My little children, these things I write to you, that you may not sin. And if anyone sins, we have an Advocate with the Father, Jesus Christ the righteous.

Our calling to God is a calling away from sin.

PROSPERITY

Another benefit of being a born-again believer – a new creation – is that we may have true prosperity. There are two types of prosperity, that of the soul, and in the financial area.

Through the apostle John, God wrote that He wants us to prosper and be in good health– even as our souls prosper.

3 John 1:2 Beloved, I pray that you may prosper in all things and be in health, just as your soul prospers.

What does God wish above all else? That we would prosper and be in good health, even as our souls prosper.

What does "as your soul prospers" mean?

Soul Prosperity

Our soul is our intellect, our emotions and our will. Soul prosperity – intellectual prosperity and emotional prosperity – comes through the total commitment of our lives as living sacrifices to Jesus, and the renewing of our minds through the Word of God. Soul prosperity is the prerequisite for prosperity and physical health.

Romans 12:1,2 I beseech you therefore, brethren, by the mercies of God, that you present your bodies a living sacrifice, holy, acceptable to God, which is your reasonable service.

And do not be conformed to this world, but be transformed by the renewing of your mind, that you may prove what is that good and acceptable and perfect will of God.

God wants His people, His new creations, to prosper in soul and body. The new creation beings are no longer to conform to this world system. They are to be conformed to God's Word.

➤ *A Process*

The new creation beings are in the process of being transformed and this transformation comes as their minds are renewed by continually reading, hearing, meditating, believing, and acting on the Word of God.

The important first step toward full health and prosperity is to come into a revelation of the new creation. This revelation will free the believer from thoughts of guilt, condemnation, and unworthiness, so that he or she will be able to receive all of the benefits of the new creation, and to begin to walk in prosperity and perfect health.

> *Described*

A truly "prosperous" child of God is described in the first Psalm.

Psalm 1:1-3 Blessed is the man who walks not in the counsel of the ungodly, nor stands in the path of sinners, nor sits in the seat of the scornful;but his delight is in the law of the LORD, and in His law he meditates day and night. He shall be like a tree planted by the rivers of water, that brings forth its fruit in its season, whose leaf also shall not wither; and whatever he does shall prosper.

A truly prosperous person is one who:

> *is walking in faith and obedience to the revelation of God's Word*

> *is walking in love and experiencing deep and intimate fellowship with God and his fellow believers*

> *is experiencing God's peace and contentment in all that he does*

> *is continually ministering unto the Lord and to the needs of others*

> *has his financial needs well provided for so that he is "well equipped for every good work"*

> *is able to give generously to the Lord and to the needs of others*

Financial Prosperity

Contrary to what we may have been taught, money is not evil. It is the love of money that is the root of evil.

Money is an important necessity in fulfilling the Great Commission. We must know how to receive God's financial prosperity so that we can reach the lost of this world with the gospel of Jesus Christ.

John did warn us that we must be careful that we don't set our affections on things of this world. We must continually be on guard against the deceitfulness of riches, or the pride of life that leads to lusting after material things, or the honor of men.

God said that if we seek first the kingdom of God and His righteousness, He would bless us with things.

Matthew 6:33 But seek first the kingdom of God and His righteousness, and all these things shall be added to you.

The new creation person who has had a revelation of righteousness, will always put the expansion of God's kingdom and God's righteousness above any need of his own. He will seek God and His righteousness, and God will give him "all these things."

> ➢ *Giving to God*

God is not looking for reservoirs in which to pour His financial blessing. Instead, He is looking for rivers, those who will be givers into His kingdom.

Jesus said,
Luke 6:38 Give, and it will be given to you: good measure, pressed down, shaken together, and running over will be put into your bosom. For with the same measure that you use, it will be measured back to you.

As we give in faith and obedience to God, He will multiply it back to us so that we can keep on giving it back to Him.

Prosperity is one of the promised benefits to the new creation. God has made a covenant of financial blessing to His people who obey Him.

HEALTH AND HEALING

Another great benefit of the new creation is God's provision for the healing of his or her body.

The revelation of the righteousness of the new creation will free some who have been bound by feelings of guilt, condemnation, and unworthiness, so that they will be able to boldly receive their healing from God.

In the redemptive work of Jesus on our behalf, He provided for our salvation for all eternity, and He also provided healing for our bodies.

Healed by His Stripes

In Isaiah's great prophecy of the coming Messiah, he spoke clearly of our healing.

Isaiah 53:5 But He was wounded for our transgressions, He was bruised for our iniquities; the chastisement for our peace was upon Him, and by His stripes we are healed.

Peter confirmed Isaiah's message when he wrote about the redemptive work of Jesus using the same words.

1 Peter 2:24 ... who Himself bore our sins in His own body on the tree, that we, having died to sins, might live for righteousness—by whose stripes you were healed.

Jehovah-Rapha

Just after the children of Israel had come out of Egypt, God revealed Himself as Jehovah Rapha, the God who is their healer.

Exodus 15:26 And said, "If you diligently heed the voice of the LORD your God and do what is right in His sight, give ear to His commandments and keep all His statutes, I will put none of the diseases on you which I have brought on the Egyptians. For I am the LORD who heals you."

God never changes. Healing is for today!

God's Word Brings Health

King Solomon tells us that life and health to a man's whole body comes through the Word of God.

Proverbs 4:20-22 My son, give attention to my words; incline your ear to my sayings. Do not let them depart from your eyes; keep them in the midst of your heart; for they are life to those who find them, and health to all their flesh.

If we give attention to God's Word and meditate on what He says about living in health, it will become a reality in our lives. As our minds are renewed, our bodies will be also.

When this revelation moves from our spirits to our minds, we will boldly speak God's Word in faith, and healing and health will become a reality.

Note: For a more in-depth study of healing read God's Provision For Healing by A.L. and Joyce Gill.

THE POWER OF GOD

Another great new creation benefit is the ability to release the power of the Holy Spirit from within us.

Negative Hindrances

Many Spirit-filled believers have failed to release the power of God which is within them because they have been held back by their negative thoughts and self-images.

Many, who have not had a revelation of the righteousness of God present in the new creation being, have been hindered by allowing sin to remain in their lives. They have been sin-conscious instead of righteousness-conscious. They have seen themselves as sinners, and have never been able to get victory in their lives. They have allowed the Holy Spirit to be grieved, or quenched in their lives.

Paul wrote,
Ephesians 4:30,31 And do not grieve the Holy Spirit of God, by whom you were sealed for the day of redemption. Let all bitterness, wrath, anger, clamor, and evil speaking be put away from you, with all malice.

A person who is sin-conscious will continue to sin, and because of this, will grieve the Holy Spirit and live a powerless, defeated life.

Revelation of Righteousness

Believers who have had a revelation of the new creation, will see themselves as righteous. They will see themselves as they were created to be. They will see themselves doing the works of Jesus. They will see themselves as righteous, having fellowship with God, and being used by Him to minister to others.

They will see themselves operating with the anointing of God manifested through their lives. Just as Jesus said, rivers of living water will flow unhindered through their lives and ministry.

Jesus said,
John 7:38 He who believes in Me, as the Scripture has said, out of his heart will flow rivers of living water.

The Power to Witness

Jesus said that the purpose of the power, which comes when we receive the baptism in the Holy Spirit, is to make us effective witnesses for Jesus Christ.

Acts 1:8 But you shall receive power when the Holy Spirit has come upon you; and you shall be witnesses to Me in Jerusalem, and in all Judea and Samaria, and to the end of the earth.

➢ *Signs and Wonders*

God's plan for reaching the lost is miracle evangelism. Signs, wonders, and miracles will always confirm the Word of the Gospel as it is shared or preached.

Jesus' final words to His believers before leaving this earth according to the book of Mark were,

Mark 16:15-20 And He said to them, "Go into all the world and preach the gospel to every creature. He who believes and is baptized will be saved; but he who does not believe will be condemned.

"And these signs will follow those who believe: In My name they will cast out demons; they will speak with new tongues; they will take up serpents; and if they drink anything deadly, it will by no means hurt them; they will lay hands on the sick, and they will recover."

So then, after the Lord had spoken to them, He was received up into heaven, and sat down at the right hand of God.

Mark 16:20 And they went out and preached everywhere, the Lord working with them and confirming the word through the accompanying signs.

Through the revelation of the new creation, believers will be able to boldly witness for Jesus Christ in the power of the Holy Spirit.

➢ *Free from Fear*

They will no longer be hindered by the fear of man.

They will boldly say,
2 Timothy 1:7,8a For God has not given us a spirit of fear, but of power and of love and of a sound mind. Therefore do not be ashamed of the testimony of our Lord ...

Believers with a revelation of the new creation will be fearless and unashamed witnesses for Jesus.

They will boldly say,
Philippians 4:13 I can do all things through Christ who strengthens me.

➢ *Unhindered Power*

The believer who has a revelation of the new creation will allow the unhindered power of God to manifest through signs, wonders, and healing miracles.

Guilt and condemnation will no longer hold him back from boldly casting out demons or from laying his hands on the sick and releasing the power of God to flow into their bodies.

A person with the revelation of the new creation will experience the benefits of fellowship with God: joy, healing and health, prosperity, and the unhindered power of God. These benefits are not to be enjoyed by the believer only. They are to flow out to a lost and dying world.

QUESTIONS TO ANSWER

1. Describe how feelings of guilt, condemnation, and unworthiness could hinder a believer's fellowship with God.

2. In what way could the revelation of the new creation and righteousness free a person to be able to receive the manifestation of his or her healing from God?

3. In what way could the revelation of the new creation and righteousness free a believer to be an effective and bold witness for Jesus?

Partakers Of The Divine Nature

THE NATURE OF GOD

When we accept Jesus as our personal Savior, we become a new creation. We receive a brand new nature. It is the nature of God Himself. How exciting it is to discover that we are actually partakers of the divine nature of God.

2 Peter 1:4a By which have been given to us exceedingly great and precious promises, that through these you may be partakers of the divine nature ...

What is the nature of God?

There are parts of the divine nature, the attributes of God, that are reserved for God alone. They are:

➢ **Eternal** – *without beginning or end*

➢ **Immutable** – *unchangeable*

➢ **Omnipotent** – *all powerful*

➢ **Omnipresent** – *present everywhere*

Imputed to Us

However, there are parts of the nature of God that are imputed to us at the moment of salvation. They become an integral part of our new creation being. We are given:

➢ **Righteousness**

➢ *Holiness*

➢ *Love*

➢ *Goodness, grace, and mercy*

These parts of the nature of God are imputed to our newly created spirit at the moment of salvation.

Revealed by His Promises

Peter wrote that by God's power we have been given all things that pertain to life and godliness. We become partakers of the divine nature by the revelation of God's Word. These have been given to us by great and precious promises.

2 Peter 1:2-4 Grace and peace be multiplied to you in the knowledge of God and of Jesus our Lord, as His divine power has given to us all things that pertain to life and godliness, through

the knowledge of Him who called us by glory and virtue, by which have been given to us exceeding great and precious promises, that through these you may be partakers of the divine nature, having escaped the corruption that is in the world through lust.

Become Partakers

It is possible to possess the nature of God in our spirit without becoming a partaker of His divine nature in our experience.

The apostle Paul wrote,
Philippians 2:12,13 Therefore, my beloved, as you have always obeyed, not as in my presence only, but now much more in my absence, work out your own salvation with fear and trembling;for it is God who works in you both to will and to do for His good pleasure.

At the moment of salvation, we possess these attributes of God in our spirits, but it is through a process of time that they work out and become part of our minds and bodies. All believers have become partakers of His divine nature in their spirits. However, it is only through the revelation of the new creation that we can become partakers of His divine nature in our souls and bodies.

Believers can become partakers and enjoy what is already theirs by the revelation of the truths which reveal they have already received the divine nature of God.

It is only as we meditate on God's Word, and by faith claim the promises of His Word, that we actually become partakers of His divine nature in our souls and bodies.

While our newly created spirits have received the imputation of His divine nature, in this lesson we will learn how to be a partaker of His divine nature in the area of our souls and bodies.

BECOMING LIKE HIM

We have been predestined in Christ to be conformed to His image.

Romans 8:29a For whom He foreknew, He also predestined to be conformed to the image of His Son ...

The new creation spirit is created in the image of God, and Christians are in the process of being conformed to His image in the area of their bodies and souls.

A Transforming Process

The Apostle Paul wrote to the Romans,
Romans 12:1,2 I beseech you therefore, brethren, by the mercies of God, that you present your bodies a living sacrifice,

holy, acceptable to God, which is your reasonable service. And do not be conformed to this world, but be transformed by the renewing of your mind, that you may prove what is that good and acceptable and perfect will of God.

As new creations, we are no longer to be conformed to this world. We are to live in a continual process of transformation as we are being conformed to the image of God's Son.

> ### ➢ *Present Bodies*

We begin the transformation process by making a total commitment of our bodies to God. Our bodies are the temple of the Holy Spirit and we are to present them as "a living sacrifice to God."

To become a partaker of the divine nature which we already have in Jesus, we must commit our lives to the total Lordship of Jesus Christ everyday.

> ### ➢ *Renew Minds*

Even as our bodies are being transformed, our souls must be transformed by a continual process called the renewing of the mind.

This transforming process takes place as we continually read, hear, meditate on, believe, and act on the Word of God. It is a supernatural work of the Holy Spirit.

By this supernatural process, our bodies and our souls become partakers of the divine nature.

God Working in Us

Paul prayed, with the intensity of a woman in labor, for the Galatian believers that Christ would be formed in them.

Galatians 4;19 My little children, for whom I labor in birth again until Christ is formed in you ...

He told the Philippian believers that God was working in them.

Philippians 2:13 For it is God who works in you both to will and to do for His good pleasure.

God continues working in the lives of His new creation beings, until they are conformed to the image of His Son.

The more we allow Him to do His work on the inside of us, the more we become like Christ.

Note: We have already studied about the righteousness of God and how it was imputed to us. Righteousness is one of the attributes of God. In this lesson, we are going to assume you know about His righteousness and how it was imputed to us at the moment of salvation and move on to the other attributes of God.

PARTAKING OF HIS HOLINESS

God Is Holy

The holiness of God is an awesome, absolute purity and perfection that is beyond description. It causes total separation from sin and impurity.

God is completely holy in His essence and in all of His ways. The angels declare His holiness.

Isaiah 6:3 And one cried to another and said: "Holy, holy, holy is the LORD of hosts; the whole earth is full of His glory!"

Commanded to Be Holy

Our new creation spirit is as holy as God Himself is holy.

The apostle Paul wrote,
Ephesians 1:4 Just as He chose us in Him before the foundation of the world, that we should be holy and without blame before Him in love.

Remember, our bodies and our souls are in the process of being conformed to the image of Christ. We must choose to be holy in our daily lives. This is experiential holiness.

Leviticus 19:2b You shall be holy, for I the LORD your God am holy.

We must choose to become holy in our conduct. We must commit our lives as holy vessels to God. We must consider ourselves dead to sin and alive to Jesus.

This is experiential sanctification, a process of being set apart from this world system and to Jesus Christ Himself. It is becoming like Jesus in our daily life and conduct.

1 Peter 1:15,16 But as He who called you is holy, you also be holy in all your conduct. Because it is written, "Be holy, for I am holy."

We are commanded to be holy and we can do this by partaking of God's nature of holiness.

PARTAKING OF HIS LOVE

God Is Love

God by His very nature is Love. He is the source of all love.

1 John 4:16 And we have known and believed the love that God has for us. God is love, and he who abides in love abides in God, and God in him.

God's greatest manifestation of love toward mankind was in the gift of His precious Son.

Romans 5:8 But God demonstrates His own love toward us, in that while we were still sinners, Christ died for us.

John 3:16 For God so loved the world that He gave His only begotten Son, that whoever believes in Him should not perish but have everlasting life.

Four Types of Love

Since in the modern world the word "love" is often misunderstood, it would be good to know the four words used for love in the Greek language.

➤ *Eros*

"Eros" is sensual love. It is not used in the New Testament. It refers to the erotic love that God has ordained between husband and wife as described in the Song of Solomon. It is forbidden by God outside of the intimate expression of love between husband and wife.

➤ *Storge*

"Storge" is a non-sensual love. It is family love or affection. It is used as the root word in the adjective "philostorgos" which means to be tenderly affectionate.

Romans 12:10 Be kindly affectionate to one another with brotherly love, in honor giving preference to one another.

Storge is the affection that family members show for one another both within natural families and within the family of God.

➤ *Philia*

"Philia" is the love of deep friendship or earnest attachment to someone. A kindred noun, "philema" means "to kiss." Philia is love of great warmth and affection.

John 5:20a For the Father loves the Son, and shows Him all things that He Himself does.

Philia was used to describe the love relationship between Jesus and Lazarus.

John 11:3   Therefore the sisters sent to Him, saying, "Lord, behold, he whom You love is sick."

Another kindred word is "Philos," which means someone very dear to one's affections.

John 15:13   Greater love has no one than this, than to lay down one's life for his friends.

This is the intimate type of love that a husband and wife have for one another (philandros).

In addition to the close and warm love relationship that Jesus had for Lazarus, it is also seen in the love relationship between David and Jonathan. It is a special love limited to a few very close relationships between two people.

➢ *Agape*

Agape love is the non-sensual love of God that is manifested as a fruit of the Spirit in the life of the believer.

Galatians 5:22,23   But the fruit of the Spirit is love, joy, peace, longsuffering, kindness, goodness, faithfulness, gentleness, self-control. Against such there is no law.

Agape love is a supernatural love. It is God's love manifested by the Holy Spirit in our hearts, through our lives, and in our actions towards others.

Since this love comes from God, it is a love that the world can only experience through the new creation – through us. It is a love for our neighbors, our friends, and as strange as it may seem to the world, and to our enemies.

1 John 3:16   By this we know love, because He laid down His life for us. And we also ought to lay down our lives for the brethren.

Summary

Eros is limited by God's laws to our spouse.

Storge is limited to our natural and spiritual families.

Philia is limited to our spouse or close personal friend.

However, through the new creation, God's **agape** love is shown to everyone, including our enemies.

Agape Love in Action

➢ *Love One Another*

By the supernatural impartation of the divine nature of God, and as a fruit of the Spirit, new creation beings have become lovers of one another.

Romans 13:8 Owe no one anything except to love one another, for he who loves another has fulfilled the law.

Jesus said,
John 13: 34,35 A new commandment I give to you, that you love one another; as I have loved you, that you also love one another. By this all will know that you are My disciples, if you have love for one another.

The thing above all others that distinguishes the disciples of Jesus is the love they have for one another.

> *A Disciple of Love*

A disciple is one who has come under the discipline of Jesus. He is more than just a Christian. He is one, who by faith and obedience, is being conformed to the love-nature and image of Jesus. A disciple will say with the apostle John,

1 John 4:7 Beloved, let us love one another, for love is of God; and everyone who loves is born of God and knows God.

The new creations, those who are partakers of the divine nature of God, will walk in God's agape love.

Romans 5:5b ... the love of God has been poured out in our hearts by the Holy Spirit who was given to us.

> *Love Commanded by Law*

The Mosaic law commanded that we love one another.

Leviticus 19:18 You shall not take vengeance, nor bear any grudge against the children of your people, but you shall love your neighbor as yourself ...

Unregenerate men and women were unable to fulfill the law. They could not in themselves love their neighbors as themselves.

Jesus gave a new commandment of love to His new creations.

Romans 13:9 For the commandments, "You shall not commit adultery," "You shall not murder," "You shall not steal," "You shall not bear false witness," "You shall not covet," and if there is any other commandment, are all summed up in this saying, namely, "You shall love your neighbor as yourself."

> *Law Fulfilled by Love*

Love is the fulfillment of the law.

Romans 13:10 Love does no harm to a neighbor; therefore love is the fulfillment of the law.

Paul wrote to the Galatians,
Galatians 5:14 For all the law is fulfilled in one word, even in this: "You shall love your neighbor as yourself."

Loving Our Enemies

God, in His great love-nature, loved us even while we were His enemies. As new creations, we too have the love nature of God. We too must love the lost of this world and share with them God's great love and compassion.

Because we are new creations, we are partakers of the love-nature of God. By the Holy Spirit, we can and must love even those who are our enemies.

Matthew 5:44 But I say to you, love your enemies, bless those who curse you, do good to those who hate you, and pray for those who spitefully use you and persecute you.

Jesus would never have commanded us to do something that is impossible for us to do. We can and must love our enemies with God's agape love.

➢ *Expressing Agape Love*

Jesus instructed His followers on how to express agape love to others – including their enemies.

Luke 6:27-30 But I say to you who hear: love your enemies, do good to those who hate you, bless those who curse you, and pray for those who spitefully use you. To him who strikes you on the one cheek, offer the other also. And from him who takes away your cloak, do not withhold your tunic either. Give to everyone who asks of you. And from him who takes away your goods do not ask them back.

The apostle Paul wrote,
Romans 12:20 Therefore if your enemy hungers, feed him; if he thirsts, give him a drink; for in so doing you will heap coals of fire on his head.

➢ *Example of Agape Love*

Stephen was a great example of supernatural agape love in action as he was stoned by his enemies.

Acts 7:59,60 And they stoned Stephen as he was calling on God and saying, "Lord Jesus, receive my spirit." Then he knelt down and cried out with a loud voice, "Lord, do not charge them with this sin." And when he had said this, he fell asleep.

We, as partakers of the divine nature, by the Holy Spirit can and must have this same supernatural love for others, even those who are our enemies.

A person who lives by his or her feelings could never experience this kind of love. It can only be experienced and manifested by those who have had a revelation of God's love within them.

➢ *Choosing to Love*

Since loving our enemies is contrary to our feelings and natural self, we who have revelation of the love-nature of God must choose to love as God loves.

1 Peter 1:22 Since you have purified your souls in obeying the truth through the Spirit in sincere love of the brethren, love one another fervently with a pure heart.

Lover of God

Those who have had a revelation of the new creation that they are in Christ, and have become partakers of His divine nature, will, above all, be lovers of God.

They will do all to please God by obedience to His Word. They will be worshipers of God.

The new creation beings will praise God continually for all his wonderful blessings. They will worship God for who He is. God's praises will continually be on their lips.

The new creations will have a deep and intimate love relationship with God.

Psalm 42:1,2 As the deer pants for the water brooks, so pants my soul for You, O God. My soul thirsts for God, for the living God. When shall I come and appear before God?

The new creation will walk in the agape love of Christ toward his fellow believers, his enemies, and toward God Himself.

PARTAKING OF HIS GOODNESS AND MERCY

God Is Good

God by His very nature is good.

Psalm 52:1b The goodness of God endures continually.

God's goodness is one of absolute perfection. His goodness is expressed toward all of His creation by His mercy and grace.

God's Mercy and Grace

God's mercy toward sinful mankind was shown most clearly and fully when He gave His Son to die in our place. One of the definitions of mercy is:

➢ *the forbearance from inflicting punishment on a law-breaker*

God's mercy is God's goodness exercised in behalf of our need. God is rich in mercy!

Ephesians 2:4 But God, who is rich in mercy, because of His great love with which He loved us ...

God is called the Father of mercies.

2 Corinthians 1:3 Blessed be the God and Father of our Lord Jesus Christ, the Father of mercies and God of all comfort.

➤ *Saved by Grace*

A definition of grace is:

➤ *God's unmerited favor toward mankind.*

It is another expression of His great love.

Ephesians 2:5,8 Even when we were dead in trespasses, made us alive together with Christ (by grace you have been saved) ...

For by grace you have been saved through faith, and that not of yourselves; it is the gift of God.

➤ *Throne of Grace*

Now, as new creations, we can come boldly to His throne of grace.

Hebrews 4:16 Let us therefore come boldly to the throne of grace, that we may obtain mercy and find grace to help in time of need.

PARTAKING OF HIS FORGIVENESS

God Forgives

The greatest expression of God's grace and mercy is found in His forgiveness. His forgiveness is extended to every sinner when they accept Jesus as their Savior – their personal substitute.

Ephesians 1:7 In Him we have redemption through His blood, the forgiveness of sins, according to the riches of His grace.

His forgiveness is extended to the believers when they confess their sin.

1 John 1:9 If we confess our sins, He is faithful and just to forgive us our sins and to cleanse us from all unrighteousness. God's forgiveness is the greatest expression of the mercy and grace of God's divine nature.

In the New Testament, forgiveness means:

➤ *to send away from*

➤ *to remit debts or sins as being completely canceled*

> *to bestow unconditional favor, by loosing from, releasing or dismissing sins or trespasses.*

God forgives and He forgets! His forgiveness is based on the redemptive work of Jesus, who not only paid the penalty of our sins, but also carried our sins away to the depths of the earth, never to be remembered or held against us again.

Hebrews 8:12 For I will be merciful to their unrighteousness, and their sins and their lawless deeds I will remember no more.

We Must Forgive

As partakers of God's divine nature, we as new creation beings, will walk in the mercy and grace of God toward others. We will forgive as God forgives.

Ephesians 4:32 And be kind to one another, tenderhearted, forgiving one another, just as God in Christ also forgave you.

> *Continue to Forgive*

Even if a person continues to sin against us, we must continue to forgive.

Matthew 18:21,19 Then Peter came to Him and said, "Lord, how often shall my brother sin against me, and I forgive him? Up to seven times?"

Jesus said to him, "I do not say to you, up to seven times, but up to seventy times seven."

As a new creation, we can forgive because we are partakers of the divine nature of God. We can and must forgive because Jesus forgave.

> *Choose to Forgive*

Forgiveness is a choice. It is an act of obedience to God. We must not wait to forgive until we feel like it. We must obey God and make a decision to forgive because God in His mercy and grace has forgiven us.

Jesus hung on the cross in the presence of His enemies. They had beaten Him, spit on Him, mocked Him, lied about Him, put a crown of thorns on His head, and even crucified Him. And yet, even as He hung on the cross, He forgave them.

Luke 23:34a Then Jesus said, "Father, forgive them, for they do not know what they do."

Jesus is our example. Because He forgave and He is in us, we too can forgive.

Forgive to be Forgiven

This same Jesus said,

Mark 11:25 And whenever you stand praying, if you have anything against anyone, forgive him, that your Father in heaven may also forgive you your trespasses.

As a new creation in Jesus Christ possessing God's divine nature of love, mercy, and grace, we too are able to forgive all who have sinned against us or against our loved ones. We are commanded to forgive so that we can be forgiven.

Conclusion

As new creations, we have the life and nature of God within our spirits. Our souls and bodies become partakers of God's divine nature as we are conformed to the image of His Son.

Our part is to present our bodies as living sacrifices to God, to spend time in God's Word, and to listen to His teachers so that our souls will be transformed by the revelation of God's Word.

We are to become partakers of God's righteousness, holiness, love, and goodness. We are to partake of His mercy and grace until we, like Him, become forgivers of others.

As new creations, our spirits received the impartation of the divine nature of God. Our souls and bodies are becoming partakers of the divine nature by the transforming power of God's Word in our lives.

QUESTIONS TO ANSWER

1. Describe the process whereby we can become partakers of God's divine nature.

2. As you become a partaker of God's divine nature, what changes can you expect in your attitude, relationships, and actions towards others?

3. Why is it important that we forgive all who have sinned against us?

Lesson Ten

God's Word And The New Creation

GOD'S WORD

Introduction

The revelation of the new creation is found in God's Word. His Word reveals Jesus and our position in Him. The transformation of our souls and bodies can only come by the renewing of our minds through the power of the Word of God.

This transformation process comes as we meditate on God's Word, visualizing ourselves as God sees us. As we begin to declare God's Word over and over to ourselves, our imaginations will begin to form God-like images. Our faith will be released and we will begin to see ourselves being, doing, and having all that God says about us as new creations in His Son.

Jesus, the Living Word

Jesus and the Word are one. To know His Word is to know Him.

John 1:1,14 In the beginning was the Word, and the Word was with God, and the Word was God... And the Word became flesh and dwelt among us, and we beheld His glory, the glory as of the only begotten of the Father, full of grace and truth.

Jesus is the Word of God, and the Word is the revelation of Jesus. Jesus is revealed in every book of the Bible. To meditate on the Word is like visiting with Jesus.

When Jesus is revealed to us, we shall be like Him!

1 John 3:2 Beloved, now we are children of God; and it has not yet been revealed what we shall be, but we know that when He is revealed, we shall be like Him, for we shall see Him as He is.

It is through understanding God's Word that we discover the life-changing revelation of the new creation.

Given by Inspiration

The Bible is authored by God. It is not only a collection of books written by various men throughout the ages, it is God-breathed and God-inspired.

2 Timothy 3:16,17 All Scripture is given by inspiration of God, and is profitable for doctrine, for reproof, for correction, for

instruction in righteousness, that the man of God may be complete, thoroughly equipped for every good work.

The original words translated "inspiration of God" means "God breathed."

When God breathed His breath into Adam, Adam became a living soul. Adam had the very life of God Himself on the inside of him.

In the same way, God breathed His life into His Word. God's Word is infallible and perfect because it is inspired by the Holy Spirit.

2 Peter 1:20,21 Knowing this first, that no prophecy of Scripture is of any private interpretation, for prophecy never came by the will of man, but holy men of God spoke as they were moved by the Holy Spirit.

Living and Powerful

God's Word is alive with the life of God. God's Word is mighty to change our lives by the power of God's Holy Spirit.

Hebrews 4:12 For the word of God is living and powerful, and sharper than any two-edged sword, piercing even to the division of soul and spirit, and of joints and marrow, and is a discerner of the thoughts and intents of the heart.

Contains Life of God

The life of God, which was breathed into the Word of God, is still as much alive with God's presence and power as it was the day it was written. The life of God, which is in His Word, continues to flow into the lives of those who spend time in it.

Proverbs 4:20-22 My son, give attention to my words; incline your ear to my sayings. Do not let them depart from your eyes; keep them in the midst of your heart; for they are life to those who find them, and health to all their flesh.

Living by the Word

The new creation lives by the Word of God.

Matthew 4:4 But He answered and said, "It is written, 'Man shall not live by bread alone, but by every word that proceeds from the mouth of God.'"

The new creation is to live in the Word, to abide in it day and night.

Joshua 1:8 This Book of the Law shall not depart from your mouth, but you shall meditate in it day and night, that you may observe to do according to all that is written in it. For then you

will make your way prosperous, and then you will have good success.

The Prevailing Word

As we read, meditate, believe, confess, and act on God's living Word, it will prevail as it did in the city of Ephesus.

Paul taught the Word of God daily in the school of Tyrannus.

Acts 19:10-12 And this continued for two years, so that all who dwelt in Asia heard the word of the Lord Jesus, both Jews and Greeks.

Now God worked unusual miracles by the hands of Paul, so that even handkerchiefs or aprons were brought from his body to the sick, and the diseases left them and the evil spirits went out of them.

As Paul continued to teach and preach the Word in Ephesus, powerful things kept happening.

Acts 19:17-20 This became known both to all Jews and Greeks dwelling in Ephesus; and fear fell on them all, and the name of the Lord Jesus was magnified. And many who had believed came confessing and telling their deeds. Also, many of those who had practiced magic brought their books together and burned them in the sight of all. And they counted up the value of them, and it totaled fifty thousand pieces of silver. So the word of the Lord grew mightily and prevailed.

If we will abide in God's Word, read and meditate on it day and night, believe, speak, and act boldly on it, the revelation of God's Word will grow mightily and prevail in our lives and our cities as it did in Ephesus and Asia Minor.

IMPORTANCE OF WORD IN OUR LIVES

Feeds our Spirit

The Word of God imparts faith to our spirits, and it builds our love for God and one another. The Word of God, feeding the spirit of the new creation, is much more important than eating natural food to feed the body.

Job 23:12 I have not departed from the commandment of His lips; I have treasured the words of His mouth more than my necessary food.

Jeremiah 15:16a Your words were found, and I ate them, and Your word was to me the joy and rejoicing of my heart

Matthew 4:4 But He answered and said, "It is written, 'Man shall not live by bread alone, but by every word that proceeds from the mouth of God.' "

Brings Approval

God expects us to study and know His Word just as Paul instructed Timothy to do.

2 Timothy 2:15 (KJV) Study to shew thyself approved unto God, a workmen that needeth not to be ashamed, rightly dividing the word of truth.

Builds our Faith

Faith comes by reading and hearing God's Word.

Romans 10:17 So then faith comes by hearing, and hearing by the word of God.

When faith comes by hearing the Word, that faith will begin to speak, confess, and declare the Word of God as truth.

MEDITATING ON GOD'S WORD

It is important that we meditate on God's Word, not on our background, deficiencies, lack of abilities, situations, or problems. If we continue to put our thoughts on these negative things, our minds cannot be renewed.

Philippians 4:8,9 Finally, brethren, whatever things are true, whatever things are noble, whatever things are just, whatever things are pure, whatever things are lovely, whatever things are of good report, if there is any virtue and if there is anything praiseworthy"meditate on these things. The things which you learned and received and heard and saw in me, these do, and the God of peace will be with you.

Meditating on God's Word is the key to being transformed by the renewing of our minds.

Psalms 1:1-3 Blessed is the man who walks not in the counsel of the ungodly, nor stands in the path of sinners, nor sits in the seat of the scornful; but his delight is in the law of the LORD, And in His law he meditates day and night. He shall be like a tree planted by the rivers of water, that brings forth its fruit in its season, whose leaf also shall not wither; and whatever he does shall prosper.

As the new creation person meditates on God's Word day and night, a transformation takes place in his or her life.

Verse three gives four results which will occur as a person continues to meditate on God's Word.

➢ **Stability:**

Their roots will have a constant supply of living water.

➢ **Fruitfulness:**

They will bring forth fruit in the proper season.

> ➤ *Dependability:*

Their leaf shall not wither.

> ➤ *Prosperity:*

Whatever they do shall prosper.

For Renewing our Minds

As we meditate on God's Word, we are "transformed by the renewing of our minds."

Romans 12:2a And do not be conformed to this world, but be transformed by the renewing of your mind ...

By meditating on the Word of God, a transformation takes place. Our souls (intellects, emotions, and wills) become transformed to be what our spirits became at the moment of salvation.

King Solomon wrote,
Proverbs 23:7a ... For as he thinks in his heart, so is he.

As we meditate on God's Word, a metamorphosis takes place. The caterpillar of our old soulish nature is transformed into a beautiful butterfly, conformed to the image of Christ Himself.

Meditation Means

> ➤ *Concentrate*

As we meditate on God's Word, we concentrate our full attention on the words that God has spoken. We repeat them over and over to ourselves.

1 Timothy 4:15 Meditate on these things; give yourself entirely to them, that your progress may be evident to all.

> ➤ *Visualize*

As we continue to meditate on God's Word, we begin to visualize the new creation. We begin to see ourselves as God sees us,

> ➤ *being what He says we are*

> ➤ *doing what He says we can do*

> ➤ *having what He says we can have*

The apostle Paul wrote to Timothy that as he meditated on the Word, his progress would be evident to all.

1 Timothy 4:15 Meditate on these things; give yourself entirely to them, that your progress may be evident to all.

Joshua wrote that first we are to meditate on the Word day and night, then we are to do what it says, and finally our way would be prosperous and we would have good success.

Joshua 1:8 This Book of the Law shall not depart from your mouth, but you shall meditate in it day and night, that you may observe to do according to all that is written in it. For then you will make your way prosperous, and then you will have good success.

As we begin to visualize Jesus as He is, understanding that we are new creations in Him, we will begin to see ourselves as He is. John wrote that we shall be like Him. What a wonderful promise!

1 John 3:2 Beloved, now we are children of God; and it has not yet been revealed what we shall be, but we know that when He is revealed, we shall be like Him, for we shall see Him as He is.

As we meditate, we will begin to speak what God's Word says about us over and over until it becomes a reality in our lives.

➢ *To Mutter*

The Hebrew word for meditate means "to mutter." As we mutter, or declare God's Word over and over to ourselves, it releases the power of God's Word into action in our lives.

Isaiah 59:21 "As for Me," says the LORD, "this is My covenant with them: My Spirit who is upon you, and My words which I have put in your mouth, shall not depart from your mouth, nor from the mouth of your descendants, nor from the mouth of your descendants' descendants," says the LORD, "from this time and forevermore."

As we mutter, or declare God's Word to ourselves, we will discover that it has become so indelibly impressed on our minds that we have memorized it.

➢ *Imagine*

As we continue meditating on the new creation truths of God's Word, it releases our imaginations to form God-like images. We begin to think God's thoughts and see ourselves as new creations through God's eyes.

Isaiah 55:8,9 "For My thoughts are not your thoughts, nor are your ways My ways," says the LORD. "For as the heavens are higher than the earth, so are My ways higher than your ways, and My thoughts than your thoughts."

> *Comprehend*

We will begin to comprehend or understand the wisdom and revelation of God.

Ephesians 1:17,18 That the God of our Lord Jesus Christ, the Father of glory, may give to you the spirit of wisdom and revelation in the knowledge of Him, the eyes of your understanding being enlightened; that you may know what is the hope of His calling, what are the riches of the glory of His inheritance in the saints.

The Word of God

There are two important words in the Greek New Testament that are used for the Word of God.

The first is Logos, which is the written Word of God. The second is Rhema, which is the spoken Word of God.

> *Logos*

Logos is the term used for the whole Bible. It is God's general words given to all of His people.

> *Rhema*

Rhema is God's Word spoken personally to me.

Rhema is the supernatural enlightenment that comes to us personally by the revelation of the Holy Spirit as we are meditating on the Logos.

When the Rhema comes, it is as though a light goes on in our spirits. We know that God has spoken personally to us. It is the Rhema Word, the Logos Word enlightened to us by the Holy Spirit, that releases our faith.

POWER OF DECLARING GOD'S WORD

The apostle Paul wrote that faith comes by hearing and hearing the Word of God. We hear the Word of God by reading it to ourselves, repeating it to ourselves, and through good teaching.

If there is a particular need in our lives, we should find the verses in God's Word that answers that need and read them again and again. Faith comes by hearing and hearing the Rhema Word of God. As we read or quote these verses over and over, they suddenly become more real to us than the situation we are in. Faith has come.

The Logos Word becomes God's personal Rhema Word as it is revealed and spoken to our spirits by the Holy Spirit. The instant we receive that revelation, faith leaps into our spirits.

Romans 10:17 So then faith comes by hearing, and hearing by the word of God.

As our understanding is enlightened by the Rhema of God, we will come into a knowledge of who we actually are in Jesus. We will be transformed into a new creation being.

Declaring God's Word

The act of declaring the Rhema of God is also called the confession of God's Word. The Greek word translated confession is "homo-logeo." To confess God's Word means:

> ➢ *To speak the same thing*

> ➢ *To agree with*

> ➢ *To be in accord with*

This is what happened to each of us when we received a Rhema revelation of the gospel. We believed and confessed that Jesus is the Son of God, that He died in our place, and that He rose from the dead.

Romans 10:9,10 That if you confess with your mouth the Lord Jesus and believe in your heart that God has raised Him from the dead, you will be saved. For with the heart one believes to righteousness, and with the mouth confession is made to salvation.

➢ *I Believe - I Speak*

The moment we believe, we are to speak, to confess what has been revealed to us. There is a spirit of faith and it says, *I believe, therefore I speak!*

2 Corinthians 4:13 But since we have the same spirit of faith, according to what is written, "I believed and therefore I spoke," we also believe and therefore speak.

➢ *Confession Misunderstood*

Many have misunderstood this truth and have tried to confess over and over something they desired. They have searched for a scripture to claim that seemed to support their desires in an attempt to coerce God into satisfying their own desires.

It is the Rhema, that which God has spoken and revealed personally to us, which will release our faith to boldly confess and claim what is rightfully ours. It is the Rhema, which we as new creations, are to boldly declare. As we speak these God-given Words, powerful things begin to happen.

God Created by Speaking

We were created in God's image. God is the Creator and He created by speaking words.

Hebrews 11:3 By faith we understand that the worlds were framed by the word of God, so that the things which are seen were not made of things which are visible.

We see God's creative power in action in the first chapter of Genesis where the phrase, "And God said," is repeated many times.

We Create by Speaking

We, as new creations, also create by the words which we speak.

Proverbs 18:20 A man's stomach shall be satisfied from the fruit of his mouth, and from the produce of his lips he shall be filled.

➢ *Power of the Tongue*

Our words can be words that bring curses on ourselves, or they can be words of life.

Proverbs 18:21 Death and life are in the power of the tongue, and those who love it will eat its fruit.

As a new creation, created in God's image, we create by words. By the power of the tongue, we release either words of life or words of death.

As new creations, we must guard our mouths and be careful what we speak. We may need to change our way of speaking. No longer should we let negative words of death or evil come from our mouths.

Declaring the Word

As we meditate on the Word of God, faith will leap into our spirits; and God will reveal His Word to us. We will then boldly declare what God has spoken in His Word.

1 Peter 4:11a (NIV) If anyone speaks, he should do it as one speaking the very words of God.

➢ *Say to the Mountain*

Jesus revealed the importance of a faith that speaks, declares the Word of God.

Mark 11:22-24 So Jesus answered and said to them, "Have faith in God. For assuredly, I say to you, whoever says to this mountain, 'Be removed and be cast into the sea,' and does not doubt in his heart, but believes that those things he says will come to pass, he will have whatever he says.

"Therefore I say to you, whatever things you ask when you pray, believe that you receive them, and you will have them."

➢ *Believe that We Receive*

When we have received a revelation of the Rhema of God into our new creation spirits, we will believe that we receive what God has spoken to us. We will begin to speak to the mountain of circumstances in our lives. The new creation person will have what he says.

DECLARATIONS OF THE NEW CREATION

Those who have received the revelation of the new creation will begin to declare their new creation rights and privileges.

Declare Boldly

I know who I am in Jesus Christ! I am a new creation! Old things have passed away! All things have become new!

I am the righteousness of God in Jesus Christ! There is therefore now no condemnation to me because I am in Christ Jesus!

I am the faith seed of Abraham. All of the promised blessings of Abraham are mine.

God has not given me the spirit of fear, but of power, and love, and a sound mind!

I can do all things through Christ who strengthens me! The works that Jesus did, I can do also! The joy of the Lord is my strength! The Word says, "Let the weak say, I am strong." Therefore, I am strong!

Surely, Jesus bore my sickness, diseases, and pains, that I don't have to bear them anymore! By the stripes of Jesus I have been healed! None of these diseases shall come on me! It is God's will above all things that I will prosper and be in health!

My God shall supply all of my needs according to His riches in glory! It is God who has given me the power to get wealth!

I have given to God, and He shall multiply His financial prosperity back to me in full and overflowing measure! Whatsoever I have sown, that shall I also reap!

I am blessed when I come in and blessed when I go out! Whatsoever I set my hand to do will be blessed by God! I will not be defeated! I am a new creation in Jesus Christ!

Conclusion

As we read, hear, study, and meditate on God's Word, faith builds in our hearts. As new creations, we begin to release the creative power of God's Word. By faith, we declare that word as we speak.

God's Word is alive and powerful. It contains the life of God. As we declare the revelation of the new creation, we become partakers of the nature of God.

As we keep on declaring the revelation of God's Word, we find ourselves, as new creations,

> *Being all that God says we are*
> *Doing all that God says we can do,*
> *Having all that God says we can have.*
> *The revelation of the new creation becomes a*
> *reality in our lives.*

QUESTIONS TO ANSWER

1. Describe how we are to meditate on God's Word.

2. Describe the difference between the Logos and the Rhema.

3. Why is it important to declare, speak or confess God's Word out of your mouth?

Courses in This Series
By A.L. and Joyce Gill

The Authority of the Believer — How to Quit Losing and Start Winning

This life-changing study reveals God's provision for mankind's victory and dominion over Satan in the world today. God's eternal purpose for every believer was revealed at creation when God said, "Let them have dominion!" You will be released into a powerful new spirit of boldness as you discover how you can start winning in every struggle of life.

God's Provision for Healing — Receiving and Ministering God's Healing Power

This powerful teaching lays a solid Word foundation which releases the faith of the students to receive their own healing, walk in perfect health, and boldly minister healing to others. Many are healed as this revelation comes alive in their spirits.

Supernatural Living — Through the Gifts of the Holy Spirit

Every believer can be released into operating in all nine gifts of the Holy Spirit in their daily lives. From an intimate relationship with the Holy Spirit, each person will discover the joy of walking in the supernatural as the vocal, revelation, and power gifts are released.

Patterns for Living — From the Old Testament

God never changes! The way He deals with His people has been revealed throughout the Bible. What He did for His people in the Old Testament, He will do for His people today! You can learn the Old Testament truths to help you understand the New Testament.

Praise and Worship — Becoming Worshipers of God

Discover the joy of moving into God's presence and releasing your spirit in all of the powerful, fresh, biblical expressions of high praise and intimate worship to God. As you study God's plan for praise and worship, you will become a daily worshiper of God.

The Church Triumphant — Through the Book of Acts

Jesus announced, "I will build my Church and the gates of hell will not prevail against it." This thrilling, topical study of the book of Acts reveals that church in action as a pattern for our lives and ministries today. It will inspire us into a new and greater dimension of supernatural living as signs, wonders, and miracles are released in our daily lives.

The Ministry Gifts — Apostles, Prophets, Evangelists, Pastors, Teachers

Jesus gave gifts to men! These precious and important gifts are men and women God has called as His Apostles, Prophets, Evangelists, Pastors, and Teachers. Discover how these gifts are being restored to His Church, and how they function to equip the saints for the work of the ministry.

New Creation Image — Knowing Who You Are in Christ

This life-changing revelation will free believers from feelings of guilt, condemnation, unworthiness, inferiority and inadequacy, to be conformed to the image of Christ. It will release each believer to enjoy being, doing, and having all for which they were created in God's image.

Miracle Evangelism — God's Plan to Reach the World — By John Ezekiel

A powerful study which will release believers into becoming daily soul winners in the great end-time harvest through miracle evangelism. Like the believers in the book of Acts, we can experience the joy of reaching the lost as God confirms His Word through signs, wonders, and healing miracles.

Many of the manuals are available in other languages.
French, Korean, Russian, and Spanish.
There are also teaching tapes and videos that go with most of them.
Call Powerhouse Publishing for more information.
1-800-366-3119